ESSENTIAL ELEMENTS for Strings

COMPREHENSIVE STRING METHOD

MICHAEL ALLEN • ROBERT GILLESPIE • PAMELA TELLEJOHN HAYES
ARRANGEMENTS BY JOHN HIGGINS

Congratulations for successfully completing Book 1 and welcome to Book 2 of *Essential Elements for Strings*! By now you are well aware of the benefits and joy of playing viola in the orchestra. The techniques you learned in Book 1 will help you reach a more advanced level in Book 2 that will make your musical experiences even more fun and exciting.

You can learn the new skills in the order they occur in Book 2, or you can master a particular skill at the time it most applies to your individual playing needs. Tabs appear on the sides of each page to help you quickly find the section or concept you need to practice.

There will be rewards for your effort! As you spend time learning more challenging material, the mastery of new skills will bring you even more joy in the years to come. Good luck, and best wishes for a lifetime of musical happiness!

Keys

D Major 2
G Major 4–5
C Major 6–7
A & D Major 12–15
F & B♭ Major 20–25
G & D minor 28–29

Rhythms

3/4 Meter 3
Dotted notes, Eighth notes/rests 8–11
Sixteenth notes, Syncopation 16–19
6/8 Meter 26–27
Mixed meter, Cut time, Triplets 30–33
Performance Spotlight 34–37
Sight-reading 38
Shifting 39
Finger Patterns 40–43
Scales 44–45
Creating Music 46
Double Stops 47
Fingering Chart 47
Index 48

To create an account, visit:
www.essentialelementsinteractive.com

Student Activation Code
E2VA-4571-0856-3856

ISBN 979-835013657-9

REVIEW

KEY SIGNATURE

Key of D

TIME SIGNATURE

4/4

NOTES

Whole | Half | Quarter

SLUR

Major Scale

A Major Scale is a series of eight notes that follow a definite pattern of whole steps and half steps. Half steps appear only between scale steps 3-4 and 7-8. Every major scale has the same arrangement of whole steps and half steps.

1. TUNING TRACK

2. D MAJOR SCALE – Round *(When group A reaches ②, group B begins at ①)*

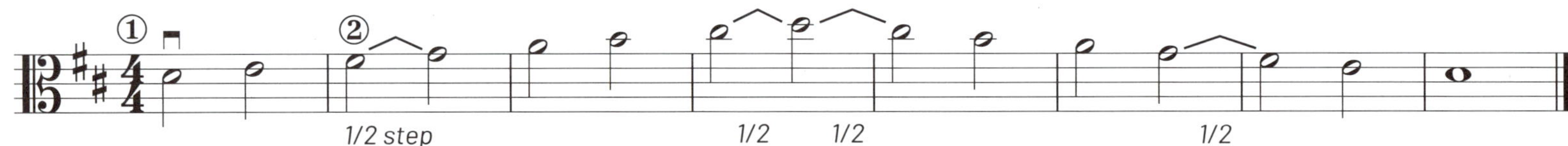

3. D MAJOR ARPEGGIO

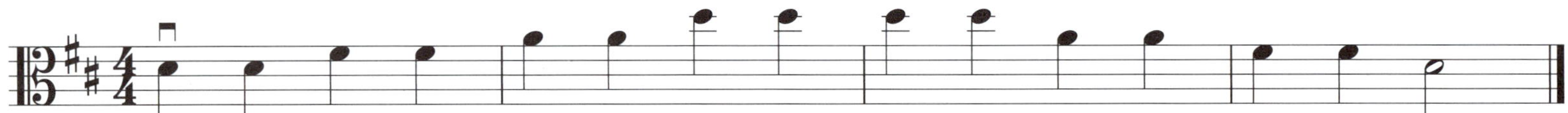

4. D MAJOR MANIA

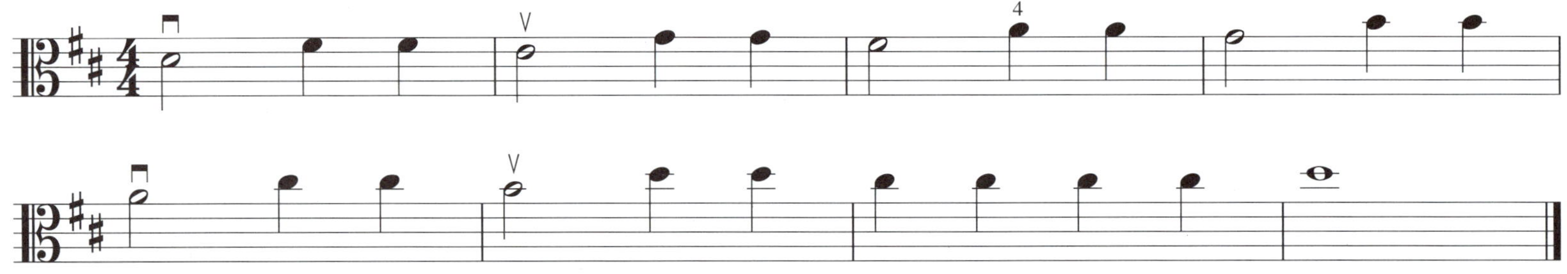

Legato

Play in a smooth and connected style. 

5. THEME FROM LONDON SYMPHONY

Franz J. Haydn (1732–1809)

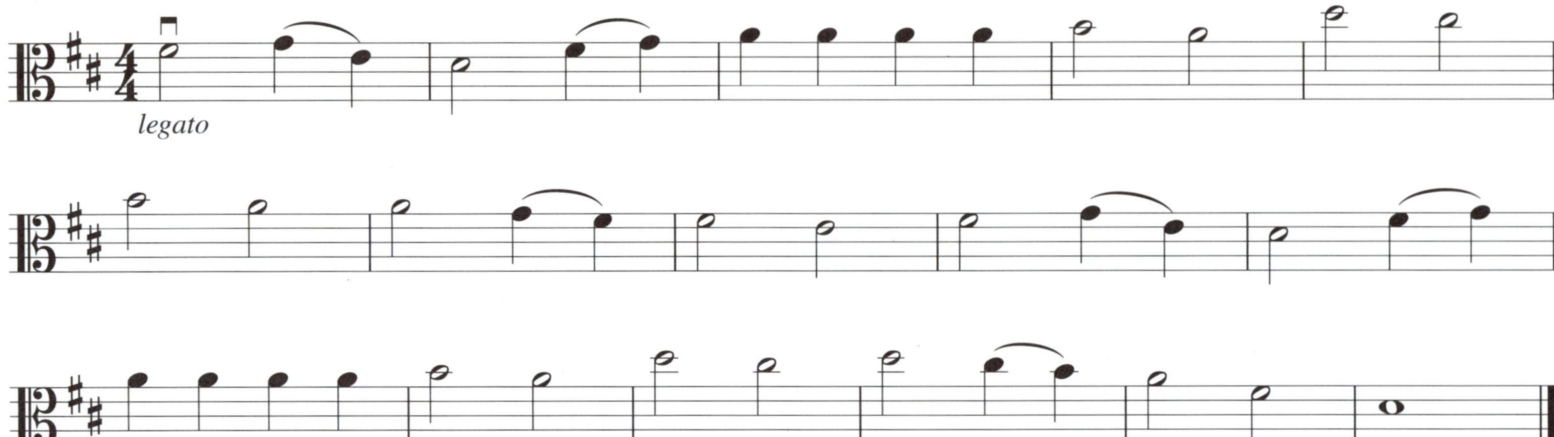

See inside front cover for information on accessing instructional videos.

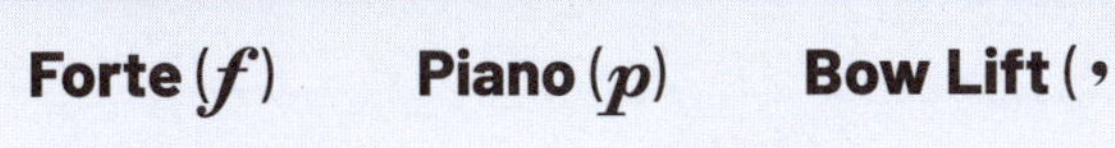

TIME SIGNATURE	NOTES		TIE	TEMPO MARKING	1st & 2nd ENDINGS
3/4	Dotted Half	Eighths		Moderato	

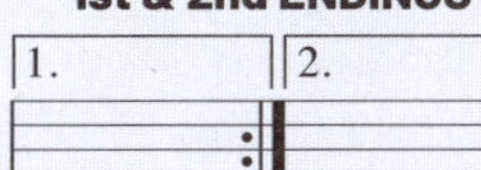

6. D MAJOR IN THREES

Dynamics

crescendo (cresc.)		Gradually increase volume.
decrescendo (decresc.)		Gradually decrease volume.

7. DYNAMIC CONTRASTS

HISTORY

Norwegian composer **Edvard Grieg** wrote *Peer Gynt Suite* for a play by Henrik Ibsen in 1875, the year before the telephone was invented by Alexander Graham Bell. "Morning" is a melody from *Peer Gynt Suite*. Music used in plays, or in films and television, is called **incidental music**.

8. MORNING (from Peer Gynt)

Edvard Grieg (1843–1907)

Moderato

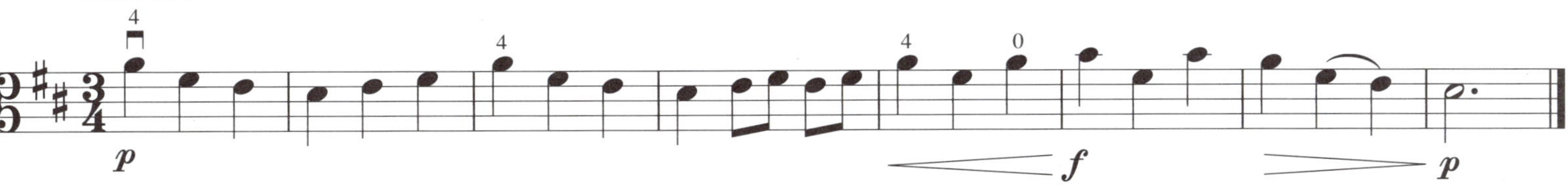

9. BARCAROLLE

Jacques Offenbach (1819–1880)

Moderato

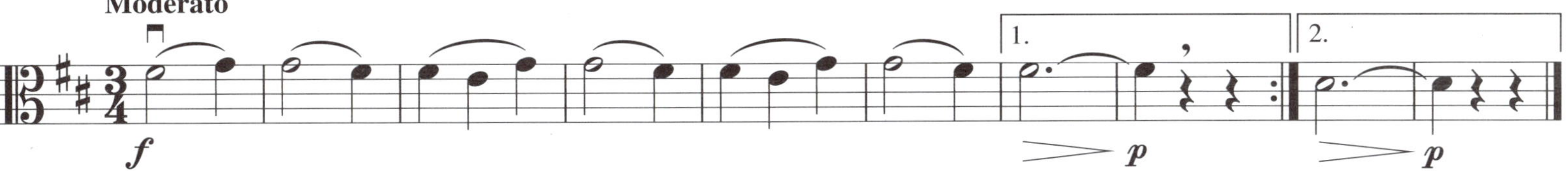

WORKOUTS

Tunneling

Slide your fingers up and down the fingerboard between 2 strings.

Ridin' The Rails

Slide up and down one string with your fingers.

Tappin' And Slidin'

Tap your fingers on any string, slide toward the other end of the fingerboard, and tap again.

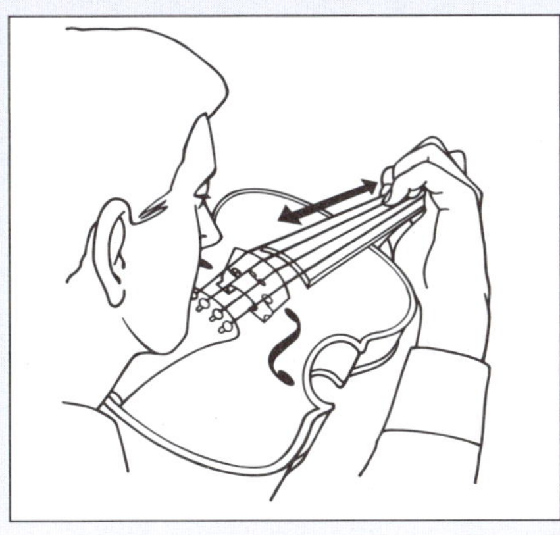

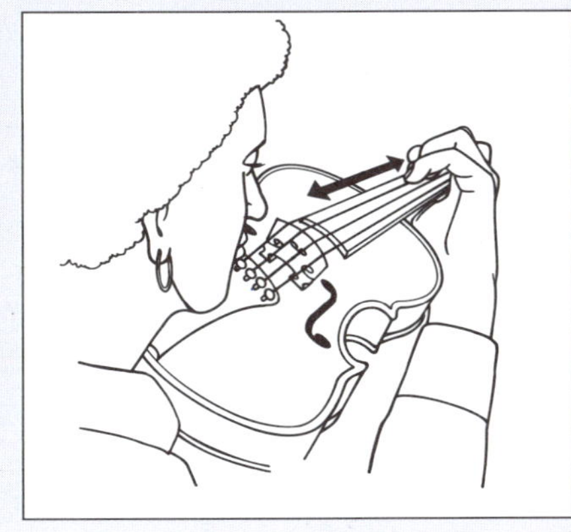

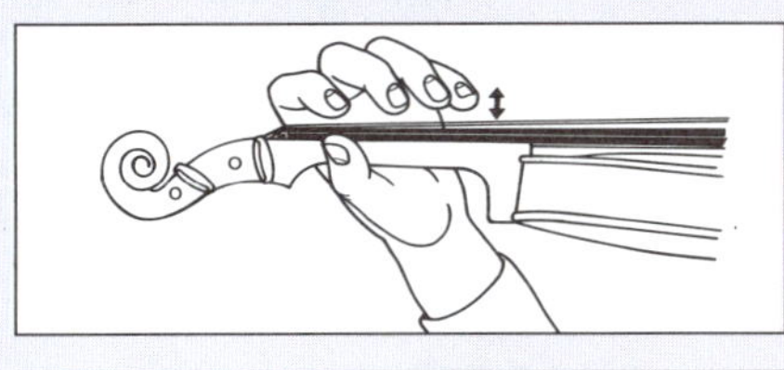

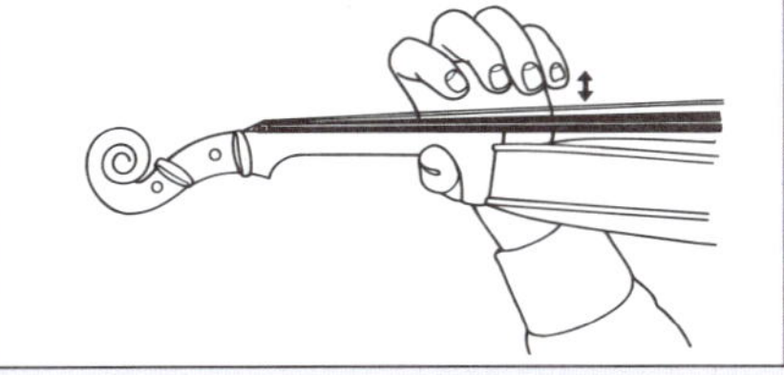

REVIEW

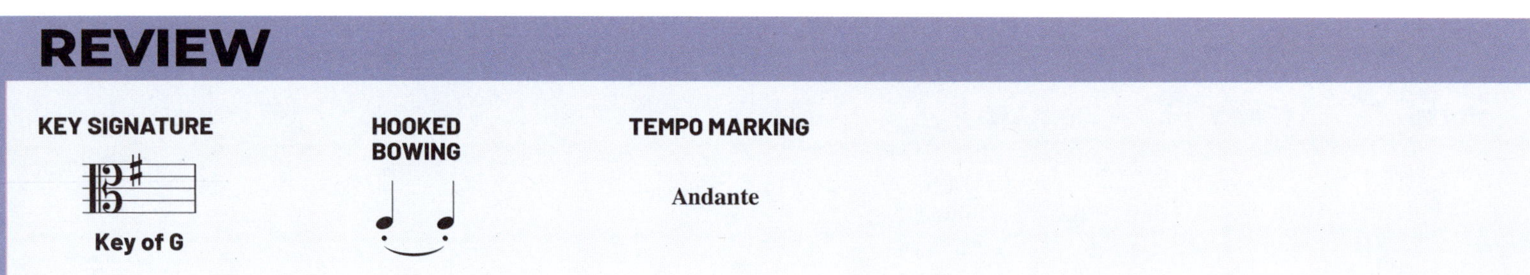

10. G MAJOR SCALE – Round

11. G MAJOR ARPEGGIO

THEORY

Interval

The distance between two notes is called an interval. Start with "1" on the lower note, and count each line and space between the notes. The number of the higher note is the distance, or name, of the interval.

12. SCALE INTERVALS

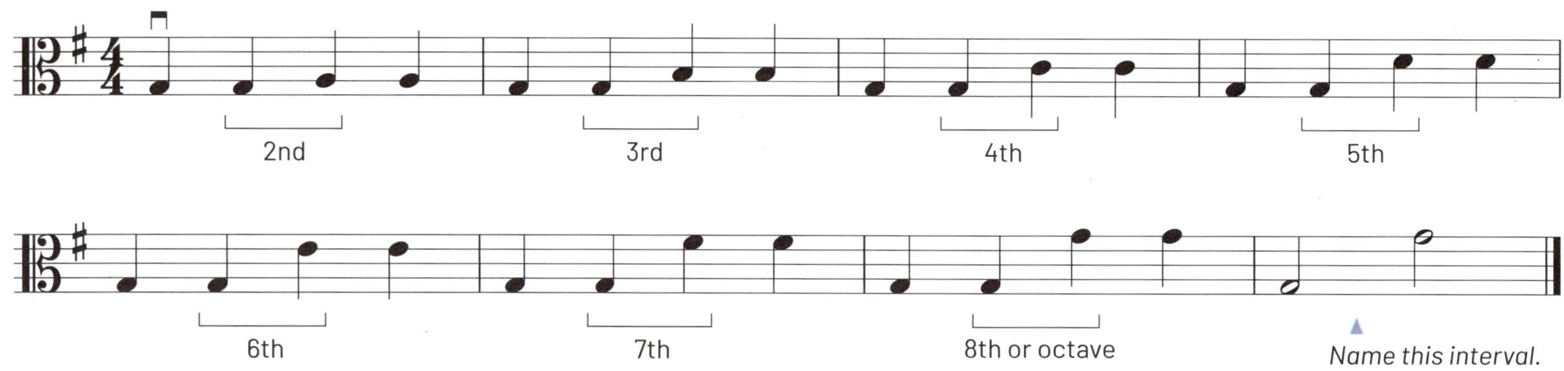

13. CHESTER

William Billings (1746–1800)

Is your left hand shaped properly?

REVIEW

KEY SIGNATURE

Key of G *(Upper Octave – violin)*

TEMPO MARKING

Allegro

14. G MAJOR SCALE *(Upper Octave – violin)*

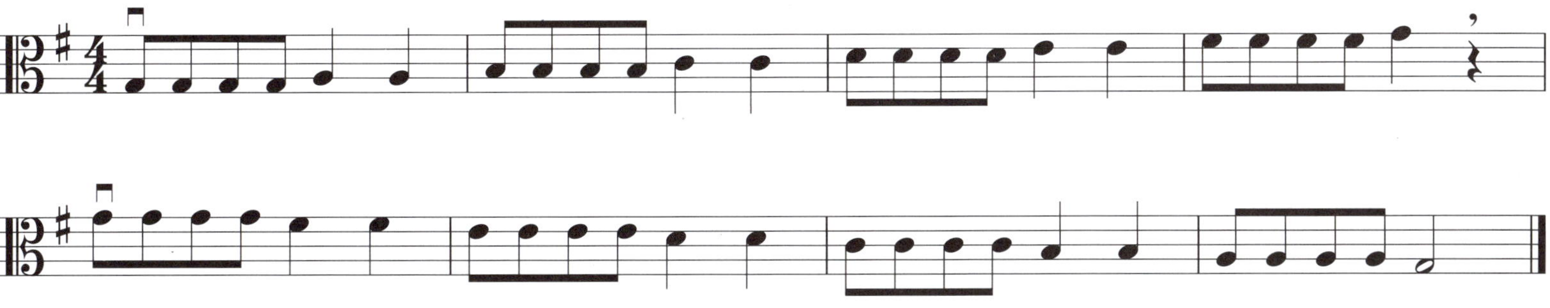

15. G MAJOR ARPEGGIO *(Upper Octave – violin)*

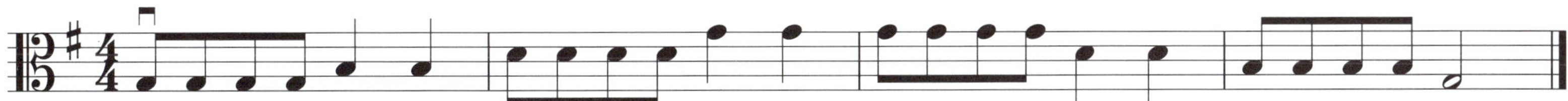

Intonation

Intonation is how well each note is played in tune.

16. INTONATION ENCOUNTER – Duet

17. THE OUTBACK

Allegro

REVIEW

KEY SIGNATURE

Key of C

TIME SIGNATURE

$\frac{2}{4}$

STACCATO

18. C MAJOR SCALE

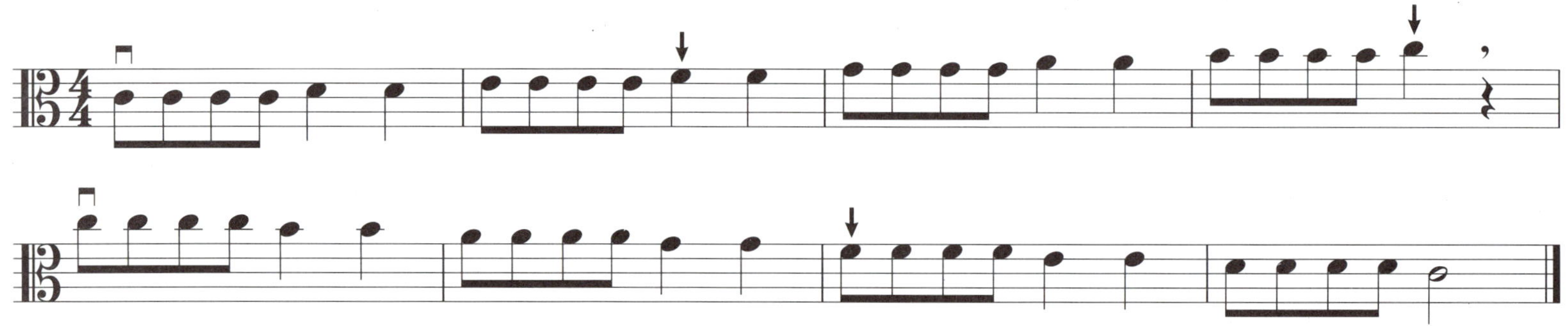

19. C MAJOR ARPEGGIO

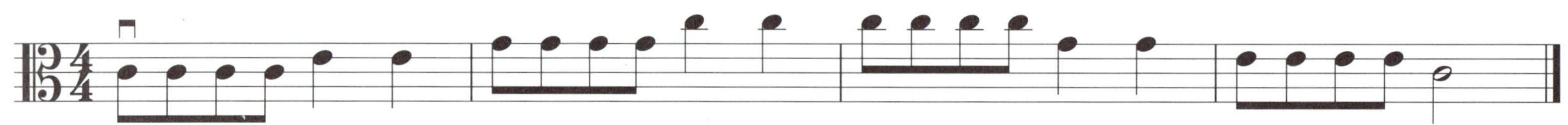

20. C MAJOR DUET

21. BINGO

Allegretto ◄ *A lively tempo, faster than* ***Andante****, but slower than* ***Allegro****.*

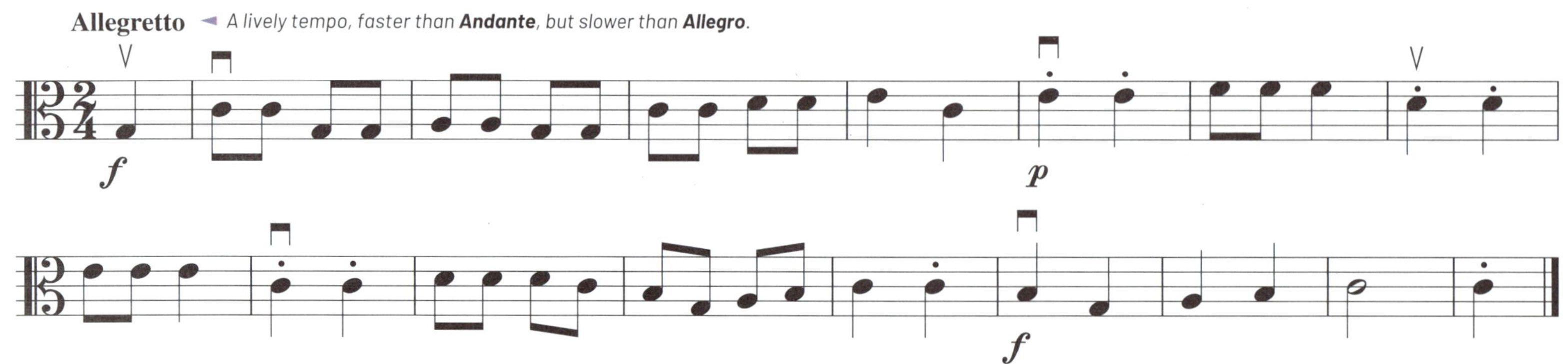

✔ Check your bow hand. Are your fingers curved and is your thumb bent?

REVIEW

KEY SIGNATURE

Key of C *(Lower Octave)*

TIME SIGNATURE

C

TONE PRODUCTION

- place bow between bridge and fingerboard
- bow straight
- proper weight

22. C MAJOR SCALE – Round *(Lower Octave)*

23. C MAJOR ARPEGGIO *(Lower Octave)*

24. C MAJOR MANIA

Dynamics

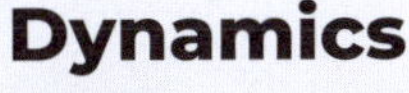

mp	*(mezzo piano)*	Play moderately soft.
mf	*(mezzo forte)*	Play moderately loud.

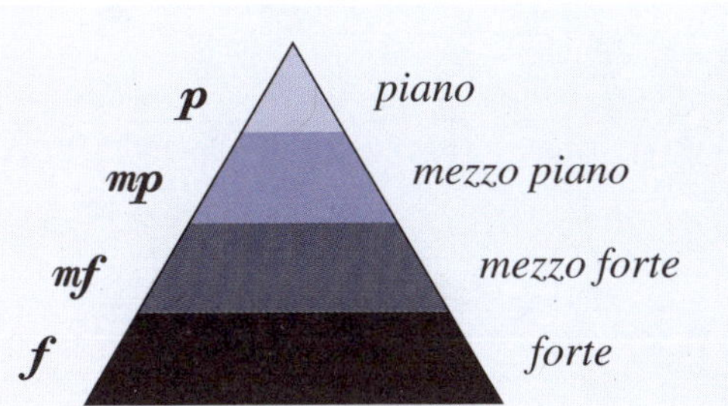

25. CROSSROADS

CHANGING BOW SPEED

Change the bow speed according to the length of the note. When you have a longer note value, the bow speed should be slower. If there is a dotted half note on a down bow and a quarter note on an up bow, the speed of the bow must change.

Example:

26. THE DOT ALWAYS COUNTS

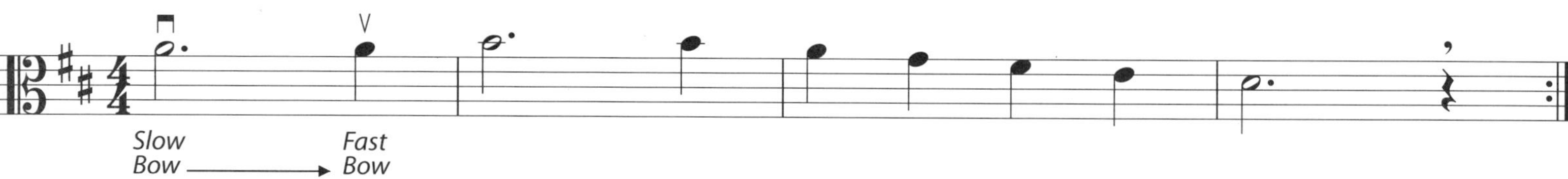

27. ALOUETTE

French Folk Song

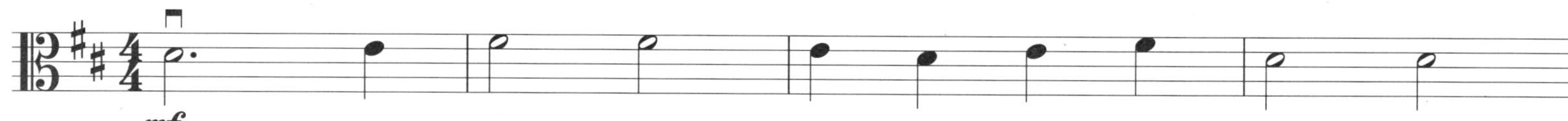

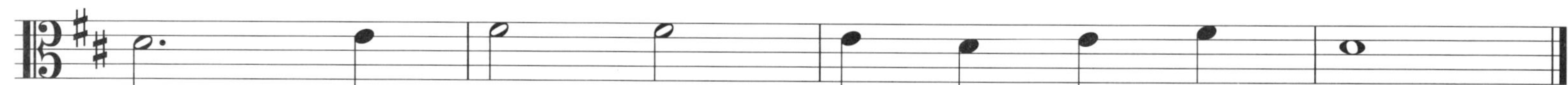

28. RIGAUDON

Henry Purcell (1659–1695)

Moderato

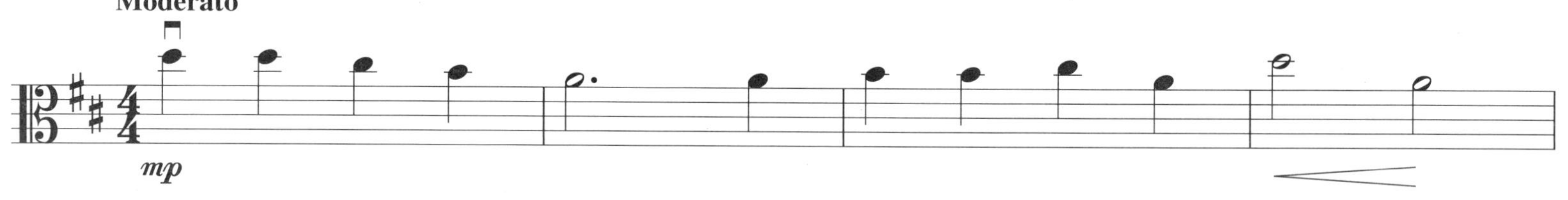

29. ESSENTIAL CREATIVITY – CANDY MOUNTAIN ROCK

Make up your own dynamics and write them in the music. Play the line and describe how the dynamics change the sound.

Allegretto

Eighth Note & Eighth Rest

♪ = 1/2 beat of sound

𝄾 = 1/2 beat of silence

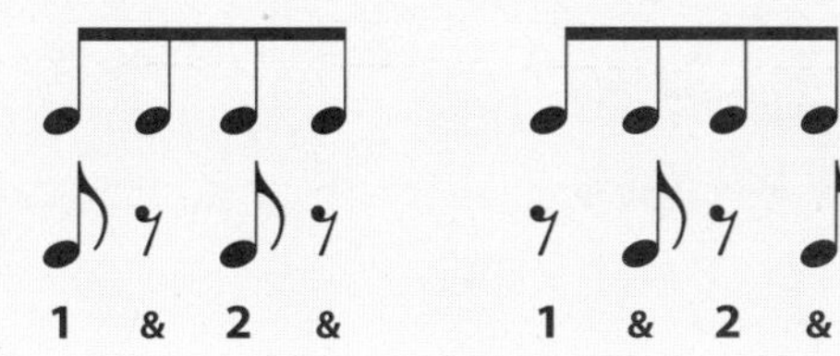

30. RHYTHM RAP ♪ 𝄾

Shadow bow and count before playing.

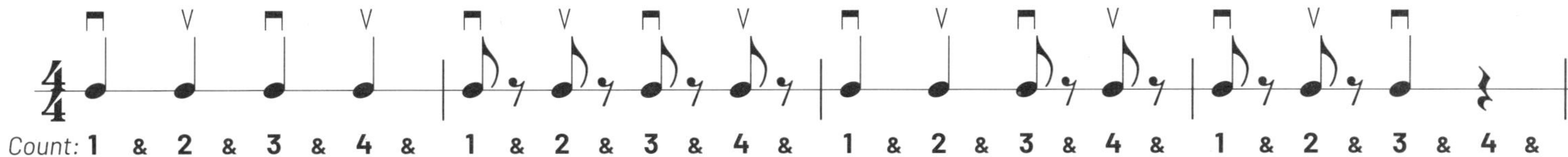

31. EIGHTH NOTES ON THE BEAT

32. SHORT AND SWEET

33. RHYTHM RAP 𝄾 ♪

Shadow bow and count before playing.

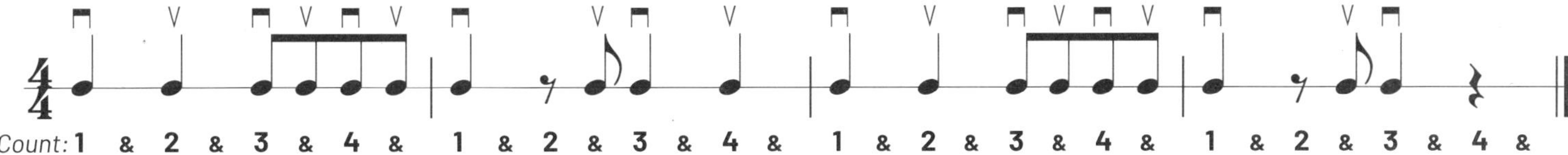

34. EIGHTH NOTES OFF THE BEAT

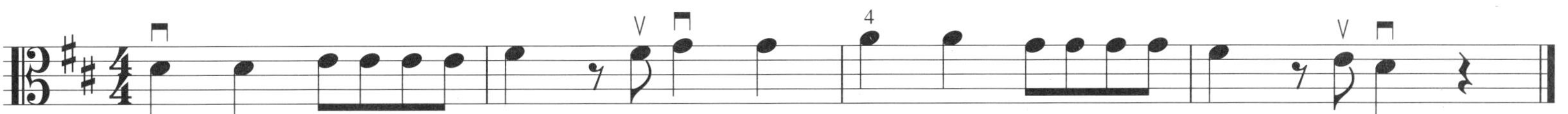

35. SUNNY DAY

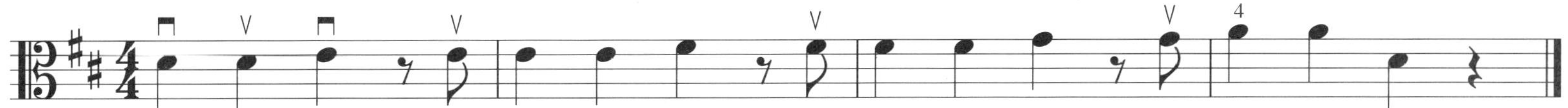

36. ESSENTIAL ELEMENTS QUIZ – JESSE JAMES

Folk Ballad from Missouri

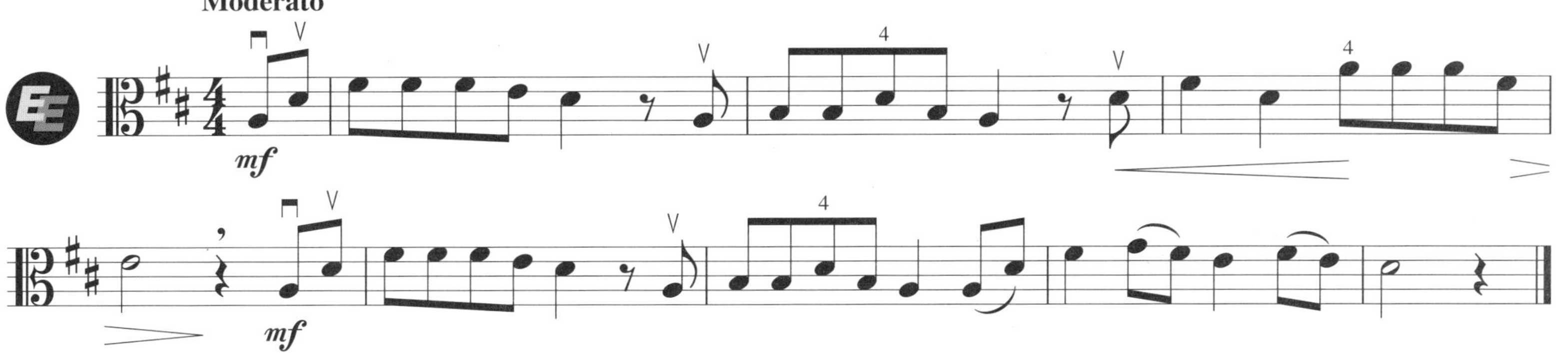

Dotted Quarter & Eighth Notes

A **dot** adds half the value of the quarter note.

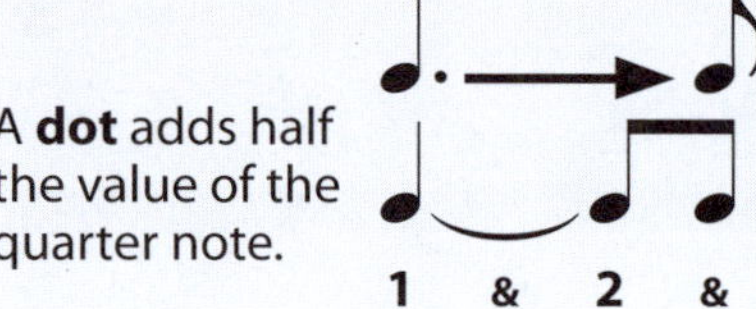

RHYTHMS

37. RHYTHM RAP

Shadow bow and count before playing.

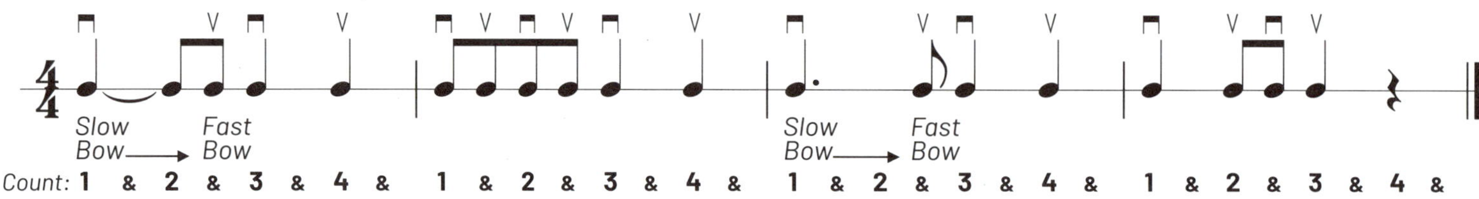

38. THE DOT COUNTS

39. WATCH THE DOT

40. D MAJOR SEQUENCE

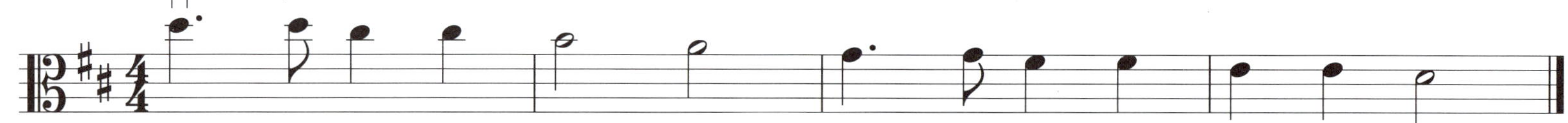

41. DOTS ON THE MOVE

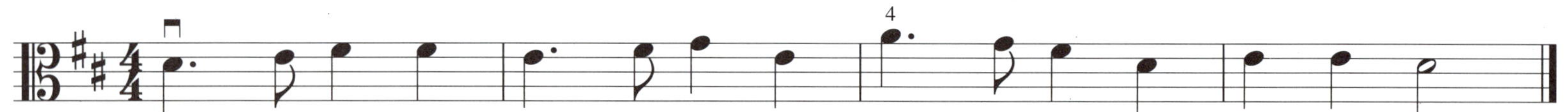

Fermata

Hold the note (or rest) longer than normal.

42. D MAJOR BONANZA – Duet

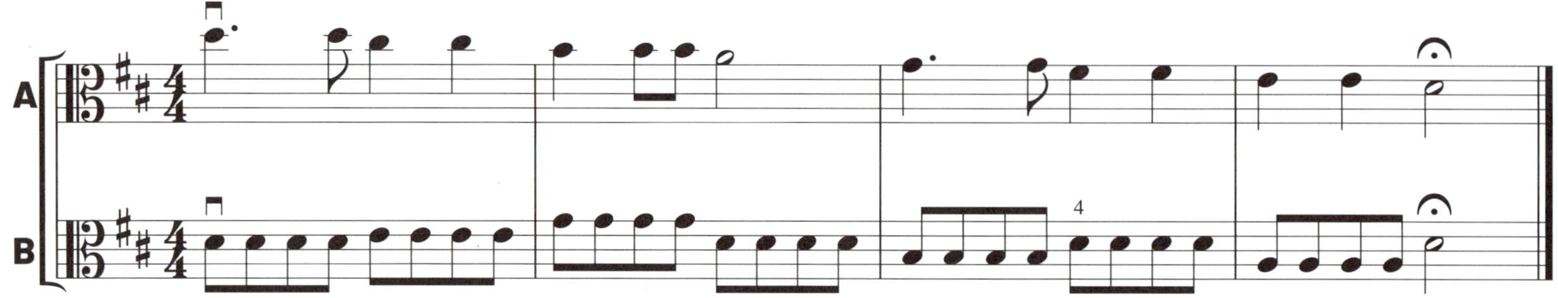

43. A CAPITAL SHIP

American Folk Song

44. ESSENTIAL CREATIVITY

Create your own rhythms by penciling in a dot and a flag to change any two quarter notes from ♩♩ to ♩. ♪

45. HOOKED ON DOTS

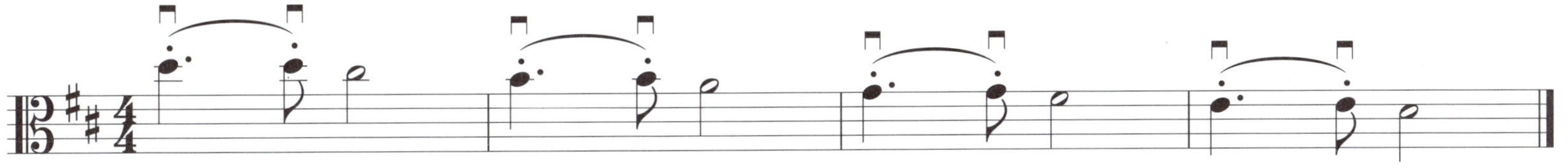

Ritardando *ritard.* (or) *rit.* – Gradually slower.

46. THEME FROM NEW WORLD SYMPHONY

Antonin Dvorák (1841–1904)

47. ESSENTIAL ELEMENTS QUIZ – RONDEAU

Jean-Joseph Mouret (1682–1738)

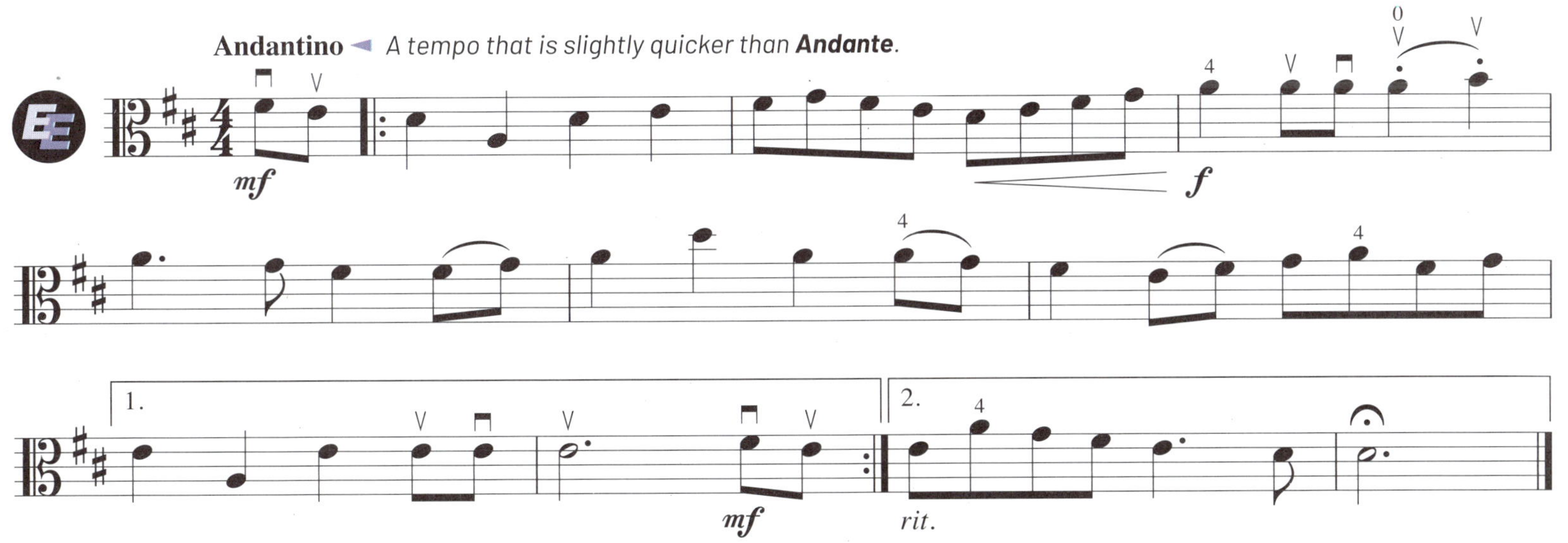

NEW FINGER PATTERN ON THE G STRING

High 3rd Finger

Step 1
Shape your left hand as shown. Be certain your palm faces you. Notice that your 3rd finger lightly touches your 4th finger.

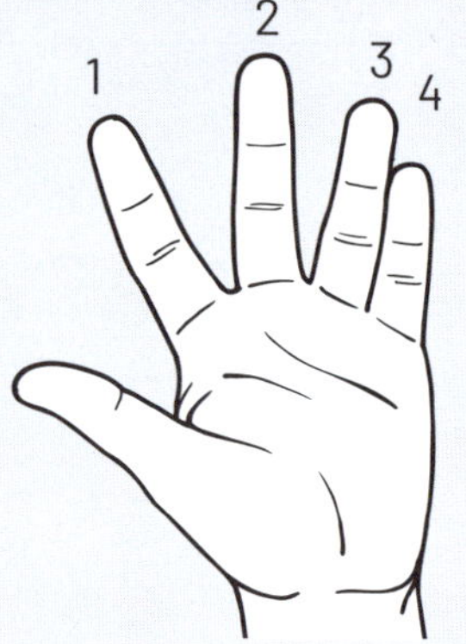

Step 2
Bring your hand to the fingerboard. Your 3rd and 4th fingers touch. There is a space between your 1st and 2nd fingers, and between your 2nd and 3rd fingers.

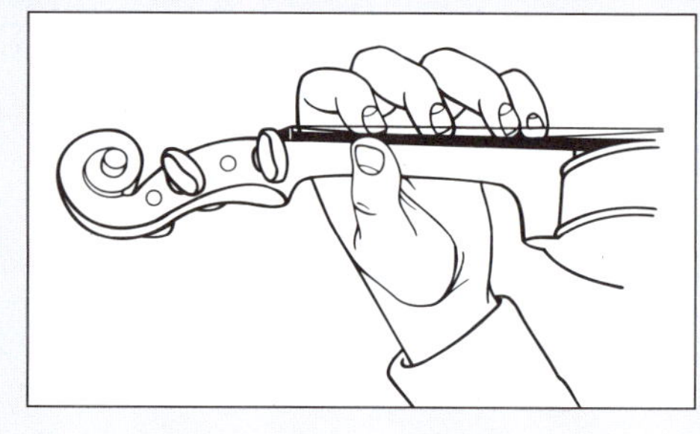

C♯

is played with high 3rd finger on the G string.

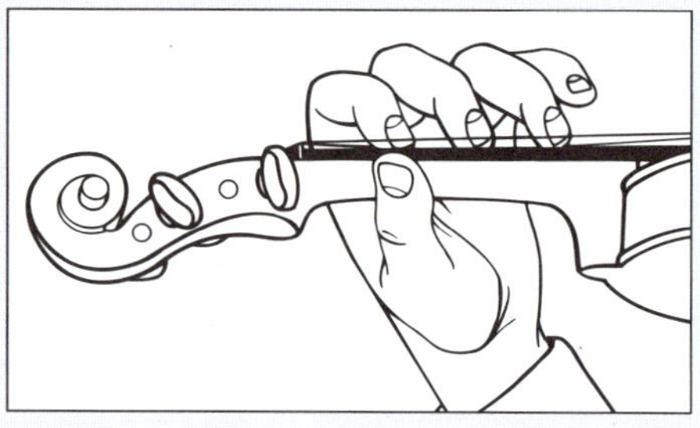

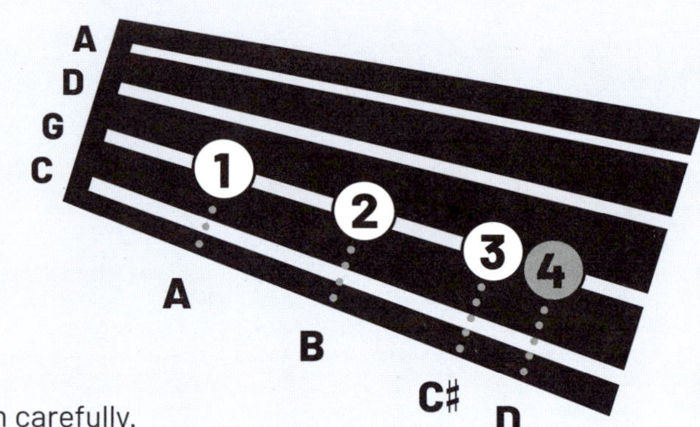

Listening Skills Play what your teacher plays. Listen carefully.

48. LET'S READ "C♯" (C-sharp)

49. STAY SHARP

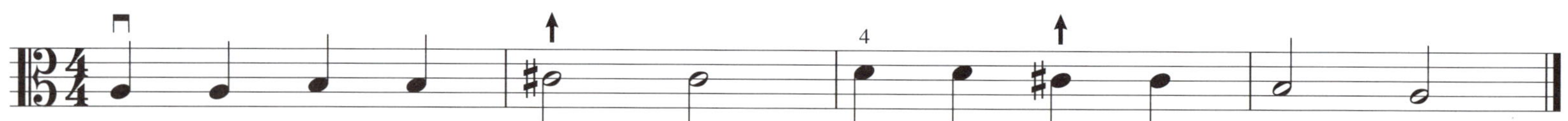

50. AT PIERROT'S DOOR

French Folk Song

51. HOT CROSS BUNS

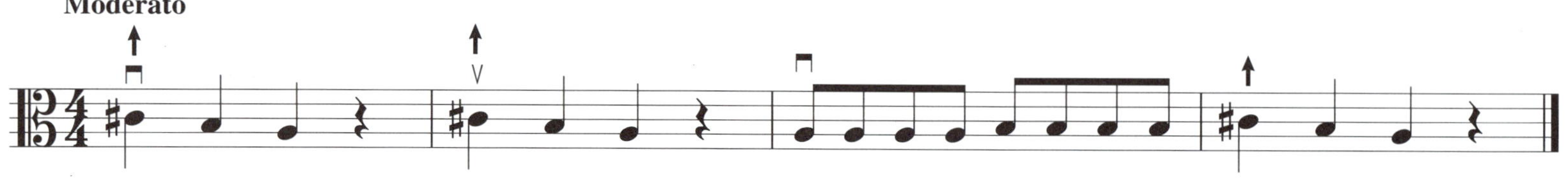

✔ Were your C♯'s in tune?

NEW FINGER PATTERN ON THE D STRING

High 3rd Finger

Shape your left hand on the D string as shown.

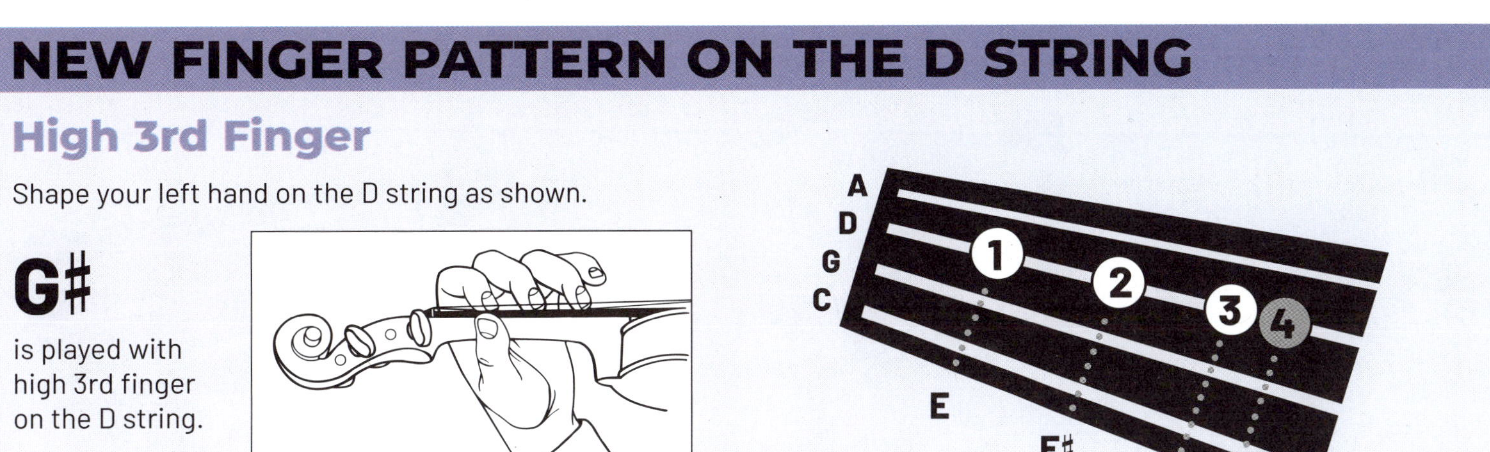

Listening Skills Play what your teacher plays. Listen carefully.

52. LET'S READ "G♯" (G-sharp)

53. REACHING OUT

54. HIGHER AND HIGHER

Key Signature A MAJOR  Play all F's as F♯ (F-sharp), all C's as C♯ (C-sharp), and all G's as G♯ (G-sharp).

55. A MAJOR SCALE

56. ESSENTIAL ELEMENTS QUIZ – A SONG FOR ANNE

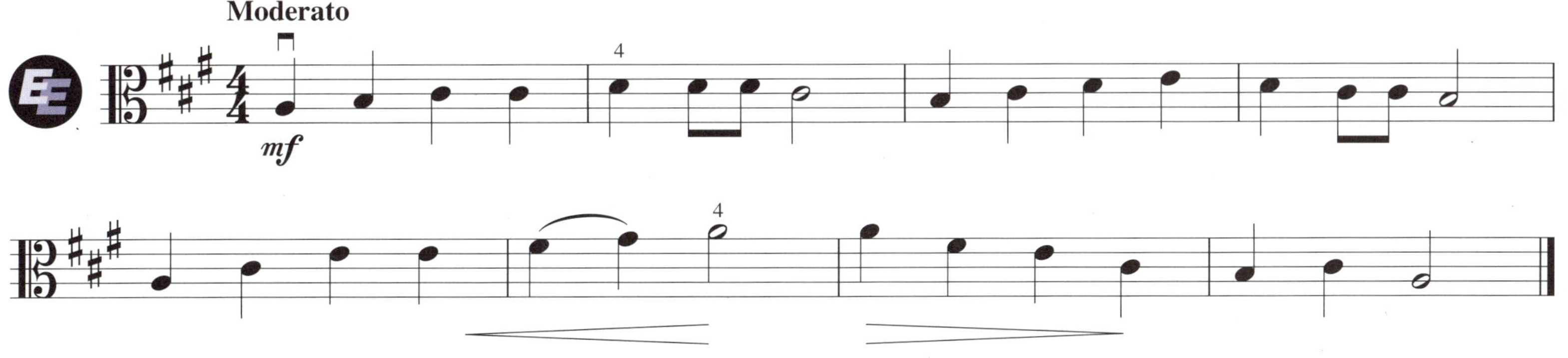

NEW FINGER PATTERN ON THE C STRING

High 3rd Finger 

Shape your left hand on the C string as shown.

F♯ is played with high 3rd finger on the C string.

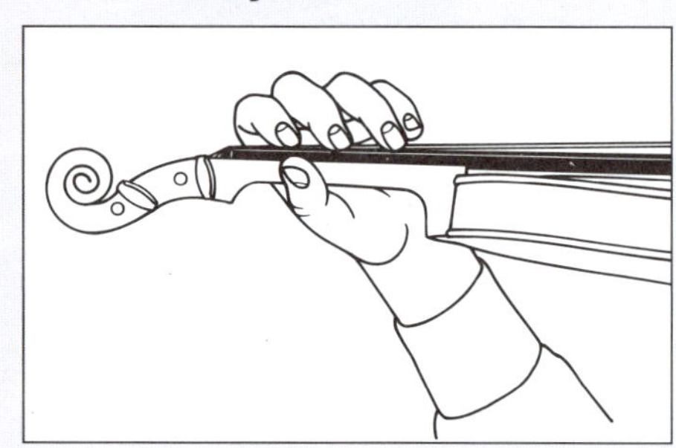

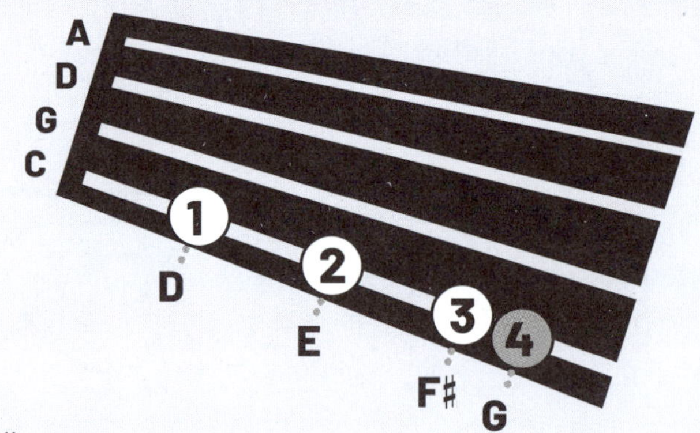

Listening Skills Play what your teacher plays. Listen carefully.

57. LET'S READ "F♯" (F-sharp) – Review

58. HIGH POINT

59. MAGNIFICENT MONTANA

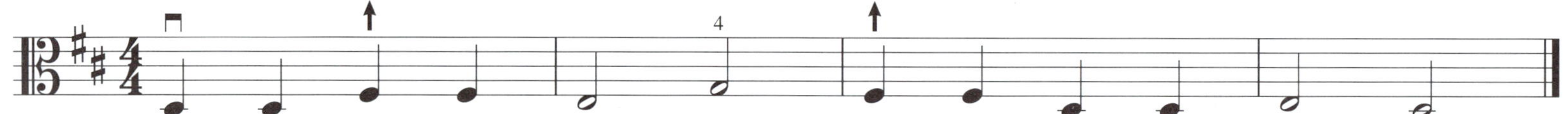

60. D MAJOR SCALE – Round

HISTORY

In the second half of the 1800s many composers tried to express the spirit of their own country by writing music with a distinct national flavor. Listen to and describe the music of Scandinavian and Spanish composers, and Russian composers such as Borodin, Tchaikovsky, and Rimsky-Korsakov. They often used folk songs and dance rhythms to convey their nationalism.

61. RUSSIAN FOLK TUNE

Special Viola Exercise

While the violins and basses are learning a new note, draw the barlines in the music below. Then write in the counting.

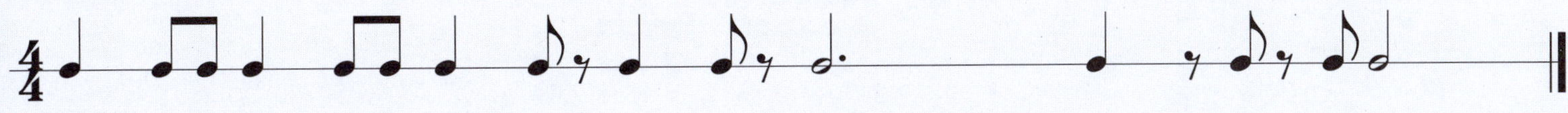

Listening Skills Play what your teacher plays. Listen carefully.

62. LET'S READ "G♯" (G-sharp) – Review

63. A MAJOR SCALE

64. A MAJOR ARPEGGIO

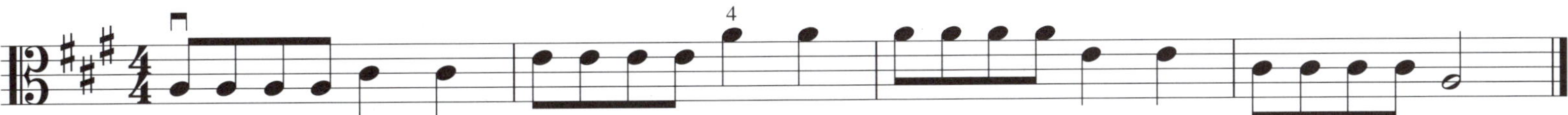

65. THE FIG TREE

Accent — or — Emphasize the note. Add weight or increase the speed at the beginning of the bow stroke.

THEORY

66. SITKA CITY

Russian Folk Song

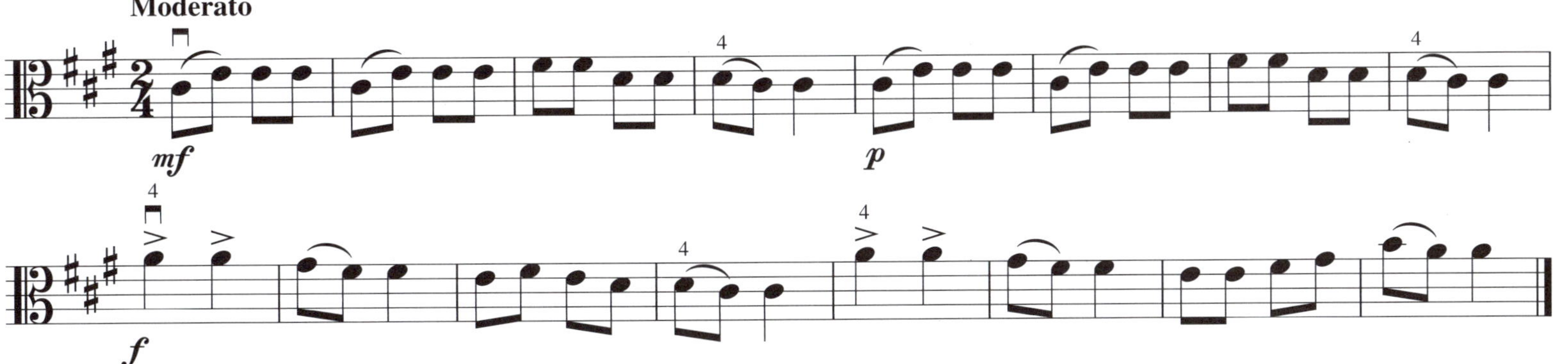

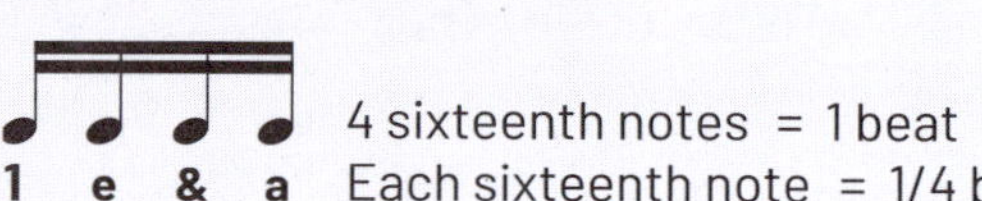

A single sixteenth note has 2 flags on the stem.

67. RHYTHM RAP

Shadow bow and count before playing.

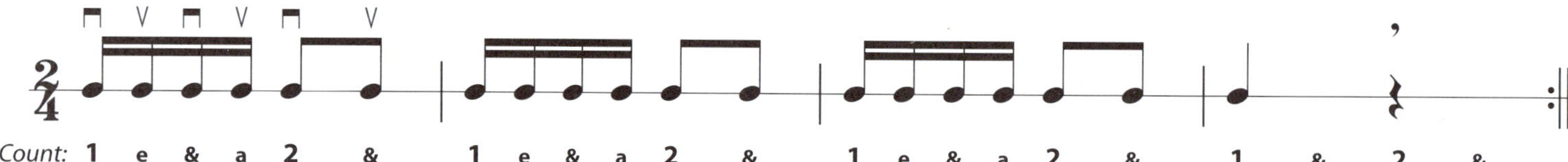

68. SIXTEENTH NOTE FANFARE

69. TECHNIQUE TRAX

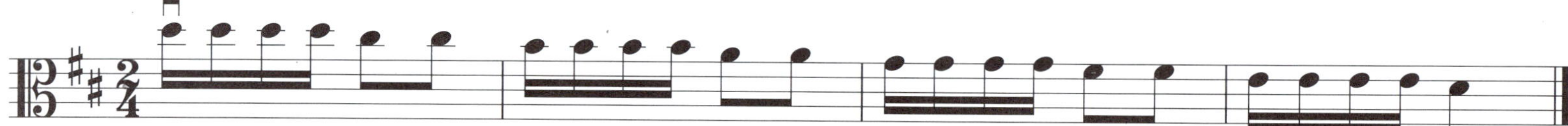

70. SWEET SIXTEENTHS

71. MOCKINGBIRD

Alice Hawthorne (Septimus Winner) (1827–1902)

Looking for some more fun music to play?
See the inside front cover for instructions on accessing recent popular Bonus Songs.

72. RHYTHM RAP

Shadow bow and count before playing.

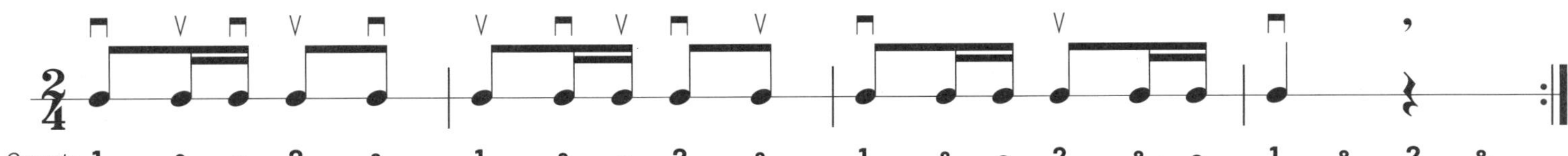

73. BLUEBERRY PIE

RHYTHMS

74. TECHNIQUE TRAX

75. RHYTHM RAP

Shadow bow and count before playing.

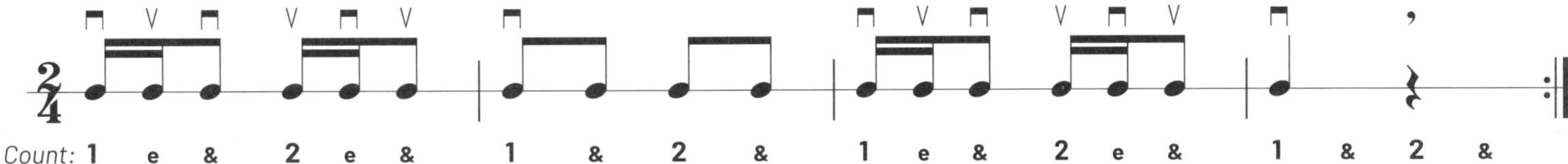

76. MARCHING ALONG

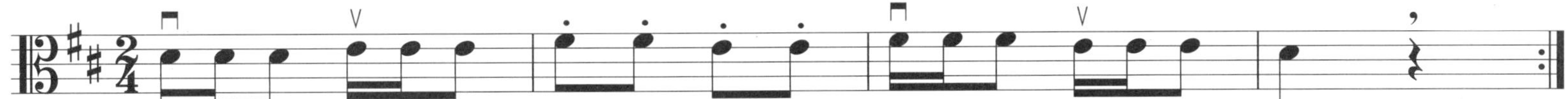

77. ON THE MOVE

78. RHYTHM ETUDE – Duet

79. ESSENTIAL ELEMENTS QUIZ – RHYTHM ROUND-UP

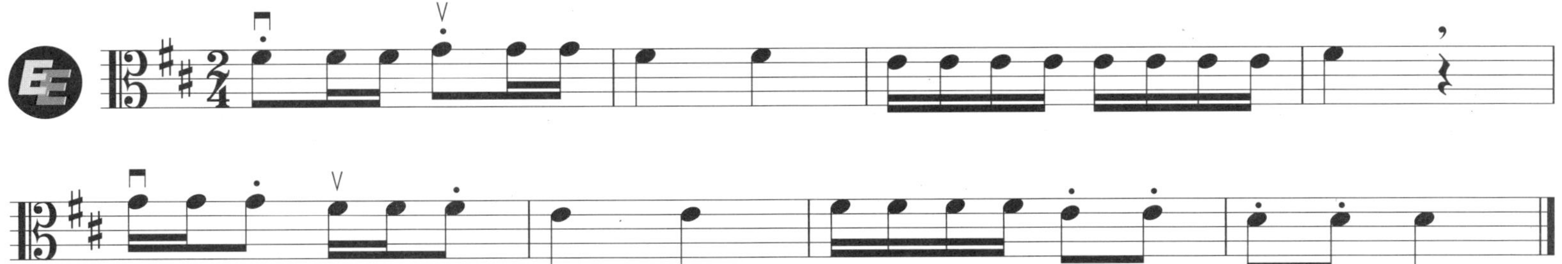

80. RHYTHM RAP

Shadow bow and count before playing.

81. TECHNIQUE TRAX

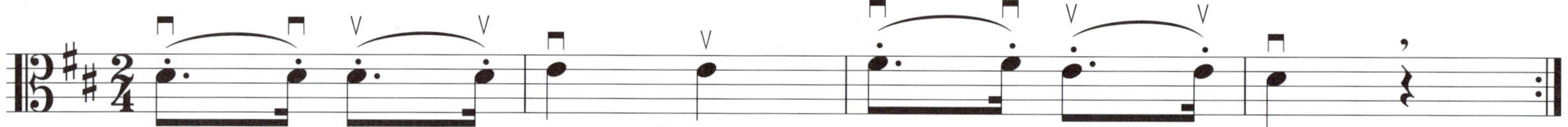

82. HOOKED ON D MAJOR

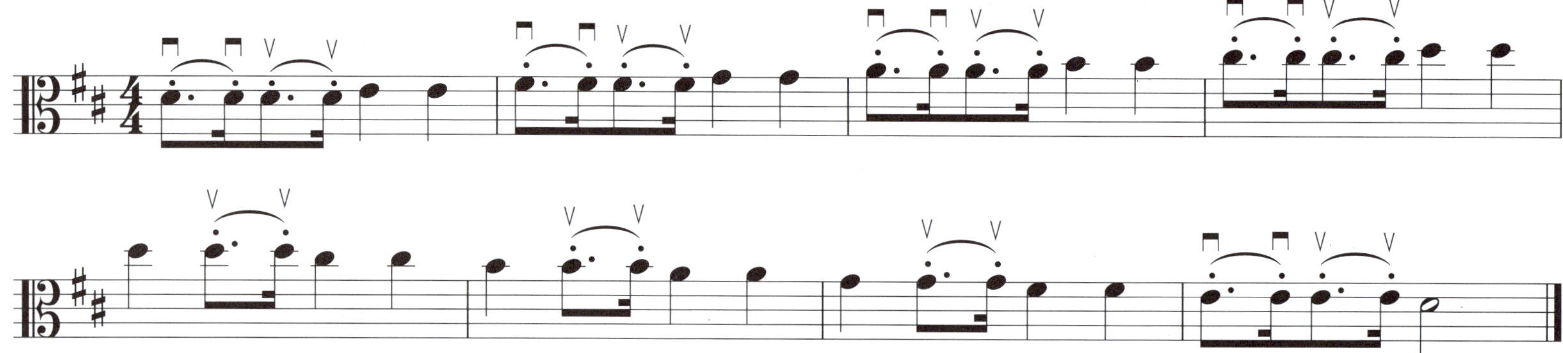

83. THE MOUNTAIN CLIMBER

84. KEEP IT SHORT

85. ESSENTIAL CREATIVITY

Write a D Major scale using any of the following rhythms: , , , *Perform your composition for the class.*

Syncopation

Syncopation occurs when an accent or emphasis is given to a note that is not on a strong beat. This type of "off-beat" feel is common in many popular and classical styles.

86. RHYTHM RAP

Shadow bow and count before playing.

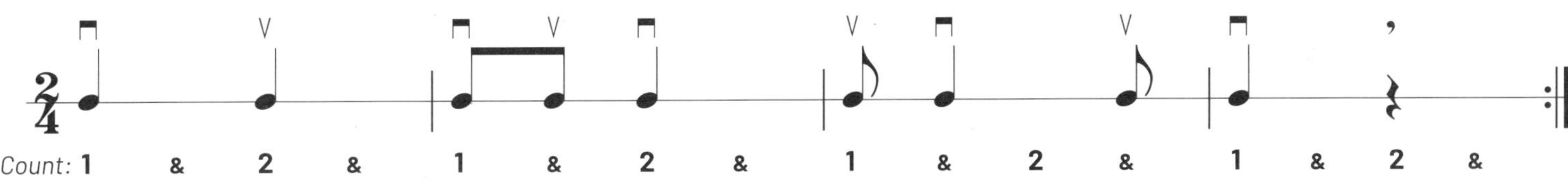

87. SYNCOPATION TIME

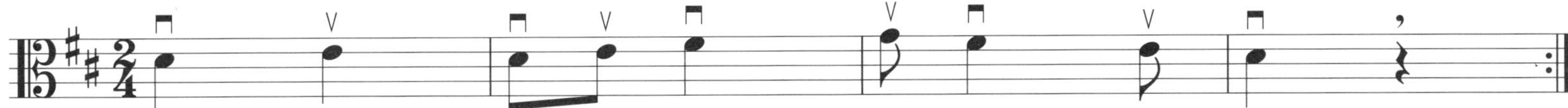

88. MIRROR IMAGE

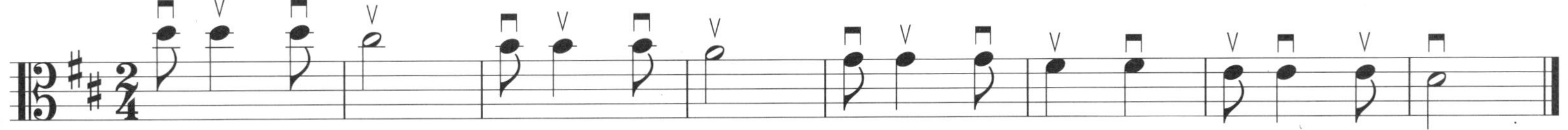

89. CHILDREN'S SHOES

African American Spiritual

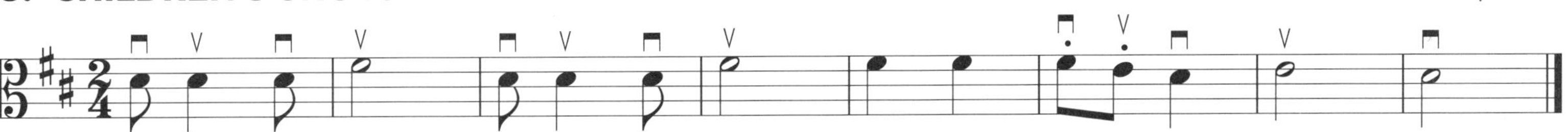

90. HOOKED ON SYNCOPATION

91. ESSENTIAL ELEMENTS QUIZ – TOM DOOLEY

American Folk Song

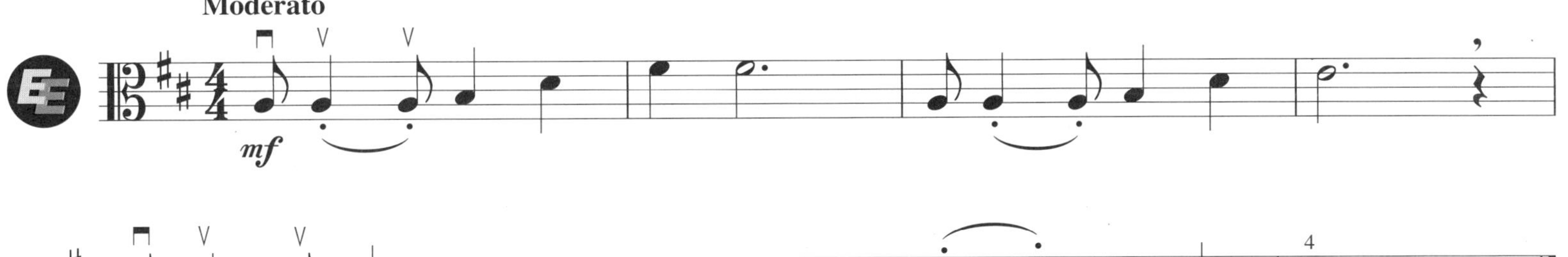

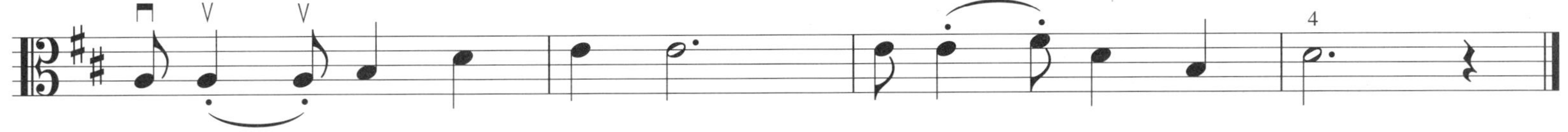

B♭ (B-FLAT) ON THE G STRING

B♭ is played with low 2nd finger on the G string.

Listening Skills Play what your teacher plays. Listen carefully.

92. LET'S READ "B♭" (B-flat)

93. ROLLING ALONG

94. MATCHING OCTAVES

Team Work Great musicians give encouragement to their fellow performers. Violin and bass players will now learn a new challenging skill. The success of your orchestra depends on everyone's talent and patience. Play your best as members of these sections advance their musical technique.

Special Viola Exercise

Draw a note next to each printed note that will match the interval number shown. The note you draw can be higher or lower than the printed note. The first one is done for you.

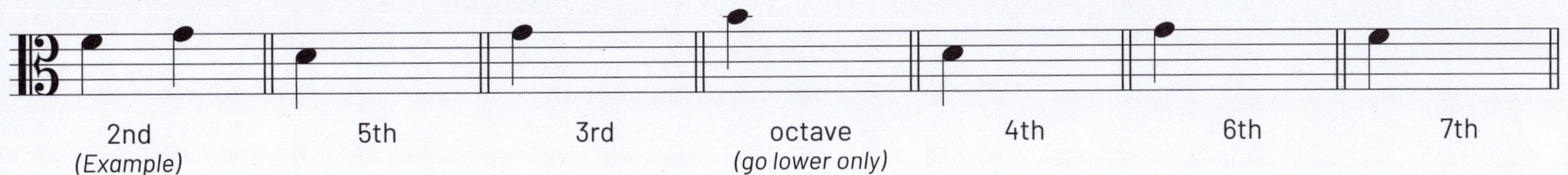

95. LET'S READ "F" (F-natural) – Review

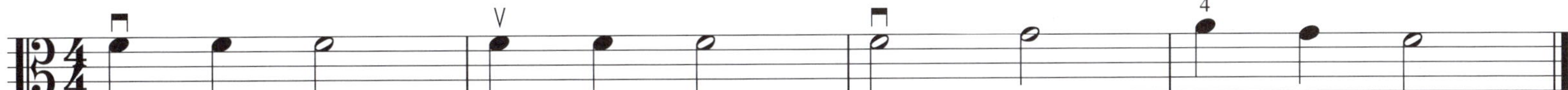

96. TECHNIQUE TRAX

Key Signature F MAJOR

Play all B's as B♭ (B-flat).

97. F MAJOR SCALE

A **Concerto** is a composition in several movements for solo instrument and orchestra. Exercise 98 is the theme from the first movement of the *Concerto for Violin and Orchestra* by **Ludwig van Beethoven**, composed while author William Wordsworth was writing his poem *I Wandered Lonely as a Cloud*. A special feature of the concerto is the *cadenza*, which was improvised, or made up, by the soloist during a concert. Improvising and creating your own music is great fun. Try it if you have not already.

98. THEME FROM VIOLIN CONCERTO

Ludwig van Beethoven (1770–1827)

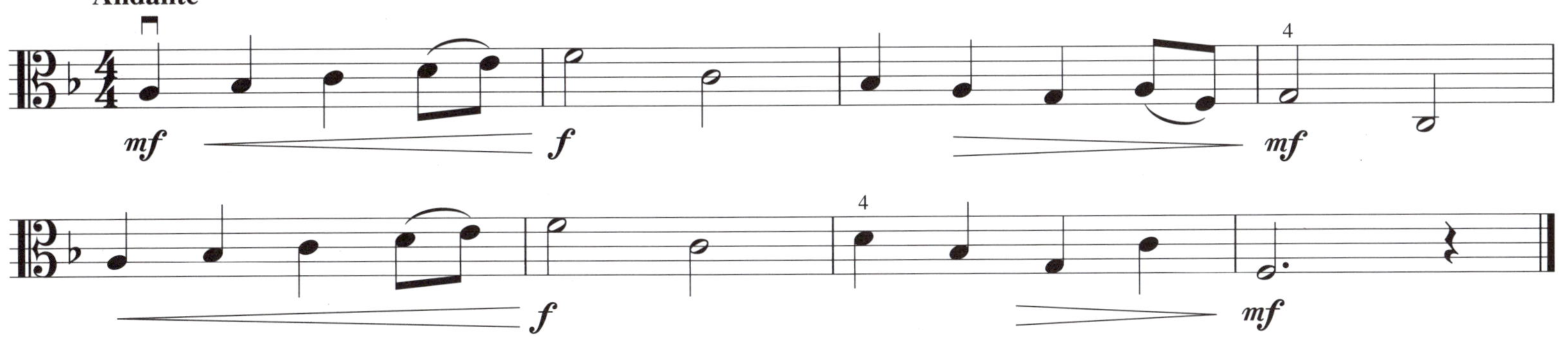

NEW FINGER PATTERN ON THE D and A STRINGS

Low 1st Finger

Step 1
Shape your left hand as shown. Be certain your palm faces you. Notice that there is a space between all four fingers.

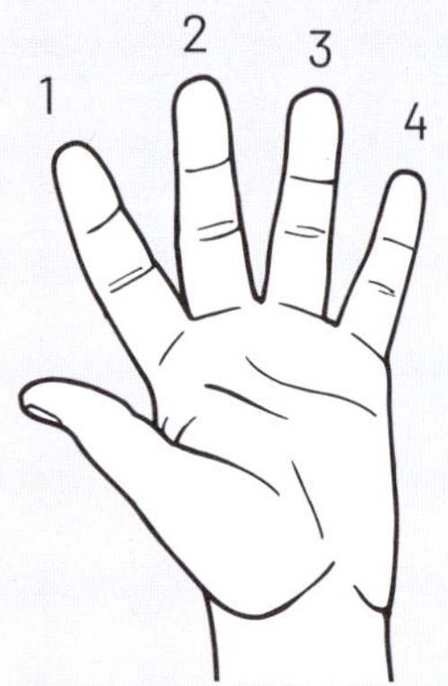

Step 2
Bring your hand to the fingerboard. There is a space between your 1st and 2nd fingers, between your 2nd and 3rd fingers, and between your 3rd and 4th fingers.

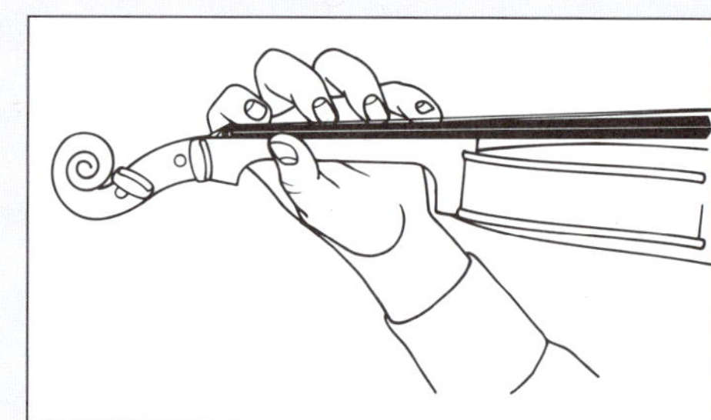

E♭

is played with low 1st finger on the D string.

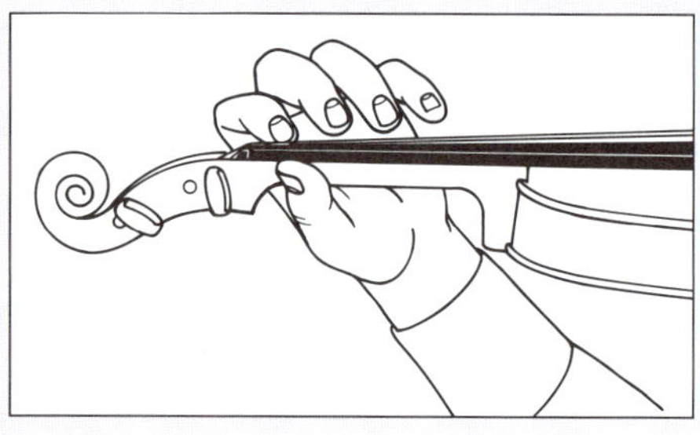

A D G C
1 2 3 4
E♭ F G A

Listening Skills Play what your teacher plays. Listen carefully.

99. LET'S READ "E♭" (E-flat)

100. HOT CROSS BUNS

B♭

is played with low 1st finger on the A string.

A D G C
1 2 3 4
B♭ C D E

Listening Skills Play what your teacher plays. Listen carefully.

101. LET'S READ "B♭" (B-flat)

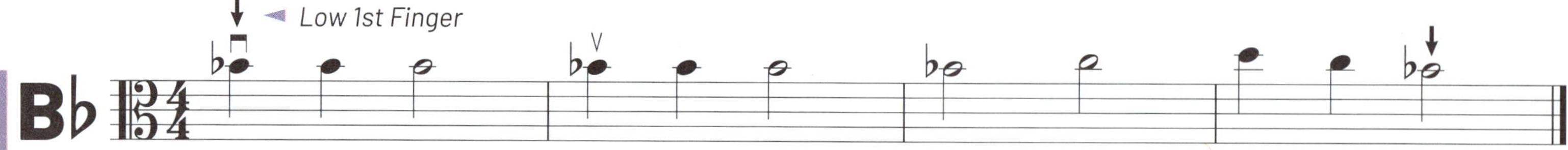

102. VIKING WAY

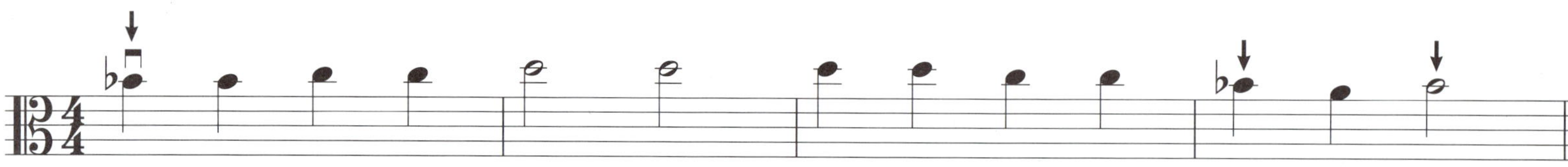

103. HIKING ALONG

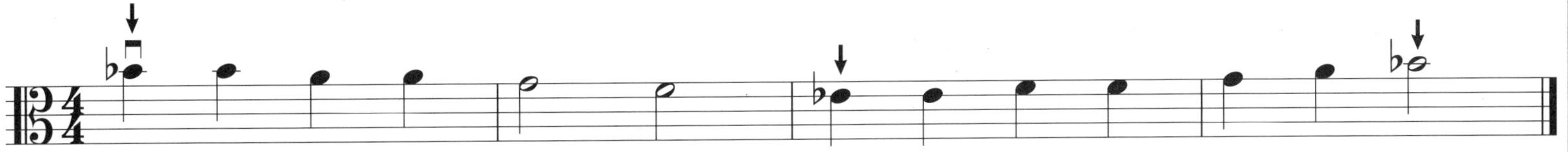

Key Signature
B♭ MAJOR

Play all B's as B♭ (B-flat) and all E's as E♭ (E-flat).

104. B♭ MAJOR SCALE

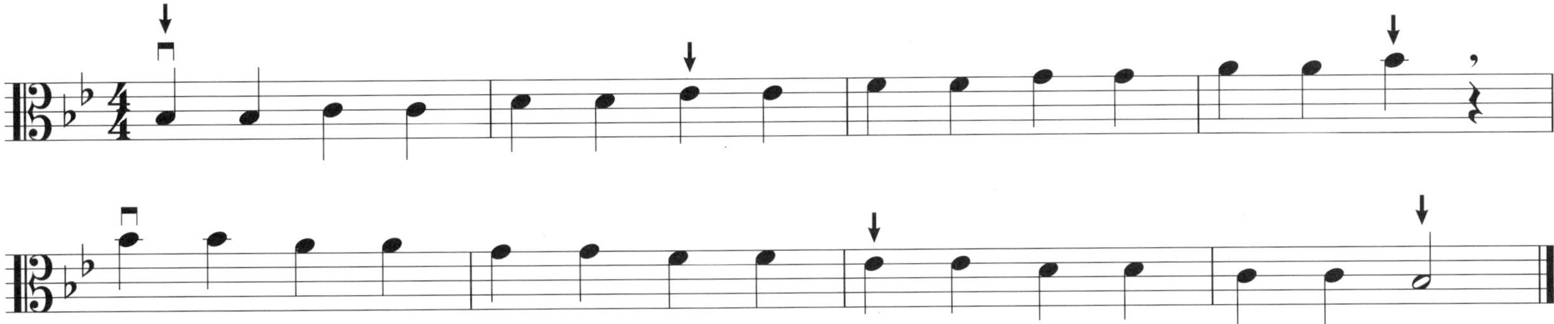

105. SLOVAKIAN FOLK SONG

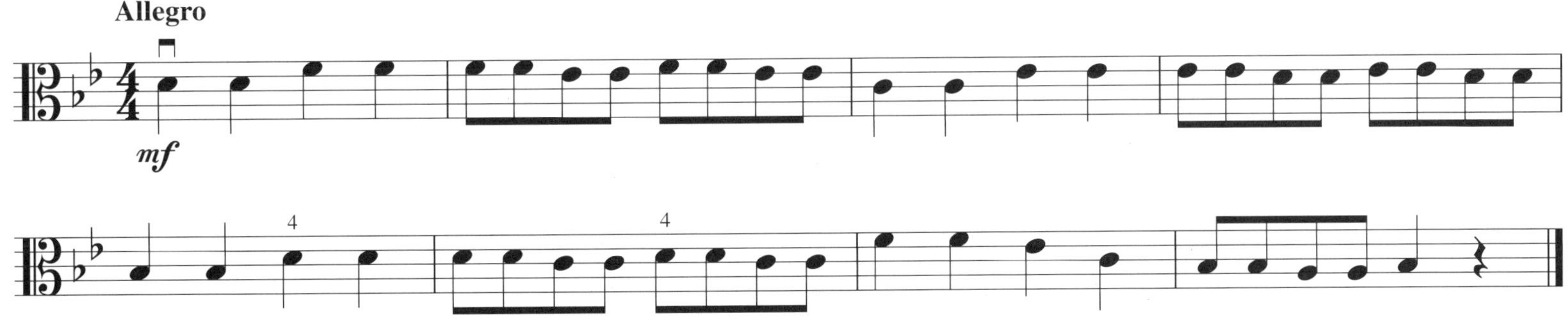

106. CAVALIER COUNTRY

107. ESSENTIAL ELEMENTS QUIZ – AYN KAYLOKAYNU

Traditional Jewish Song

NEW FINGER PATTERN ON THE A STRING

Low 4th Finger

Step 1
Shape your left hand as shown. Be certain your palm faces you. Notice that your 3rd and 4th fingers lightly touch.

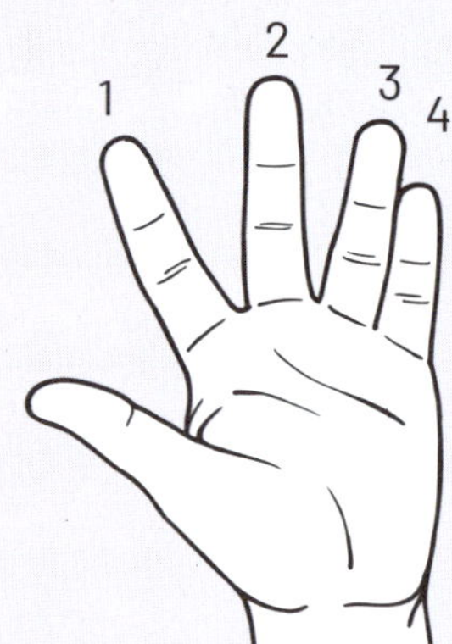

Step 2
Bring your hand to the fingerboard. Your 3rd and 4th fingers touch. There is a space between your 1st and 2nd fingers, and between your 2nd and 3rd fingers.

E♭ is played with low 4th finger on the A string.

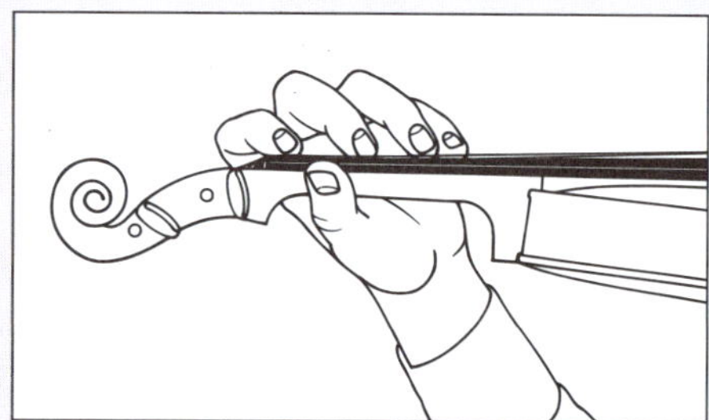

A D G C
1 2 3 4
B♭ C D E♭

Listening Skills Play what your teacher plays. Listen carefully.

108. LET'S READ "E♭" (E-flat)

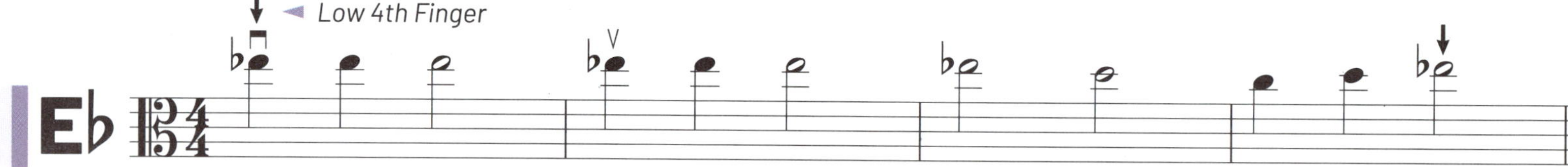

109. TECHNIQUE TRAX

110. LET'S READ "B♭" (B-flat)

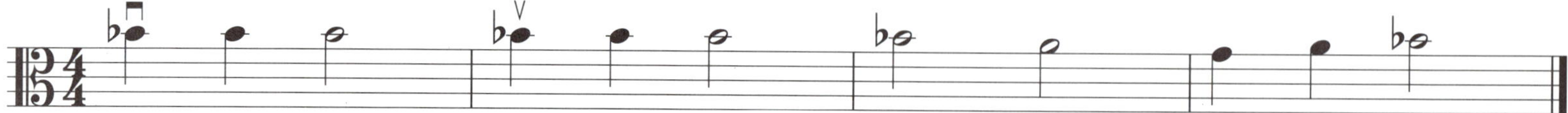

111. TECHNIQUE BUILDER

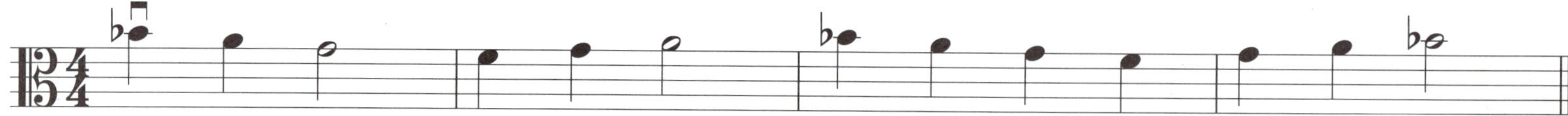

112. B♭ MAJOR SCALE

113. THE MOUNTAIN DEER CHASE

North American Folk Song

114. ESSENTIAL CREATIVITY – RAKES OF MALLOW

Irish Folk Song

Music can be created and arranged by changing rhythms and notes to an existing example. Create your own arrangement of *Rakes of Mallow* by changing the rhythms and melodic phrases. Perform your arrangement for others.

Example 1: Changing rhythms

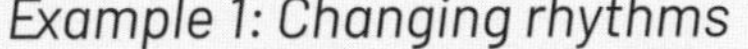

Example 2: Changing melodic phrases

THEORY

6/8 Time Signature

6/8 = **6 beats** per measure
= **Eighth** note gets one beat

♪ = 1 beat ♩ = 2 beats
♩. = 3 beats 𝅗𝅥. = 6 beats

6/8 time is usually played with a slight emphasis on the **1st** and **4th** beats of each measure. This divides the measure into 2 groups of 3 beats each.

6/8 RHYTHMS

115. RHYTHM RAP

Shadow bow and count before playing.

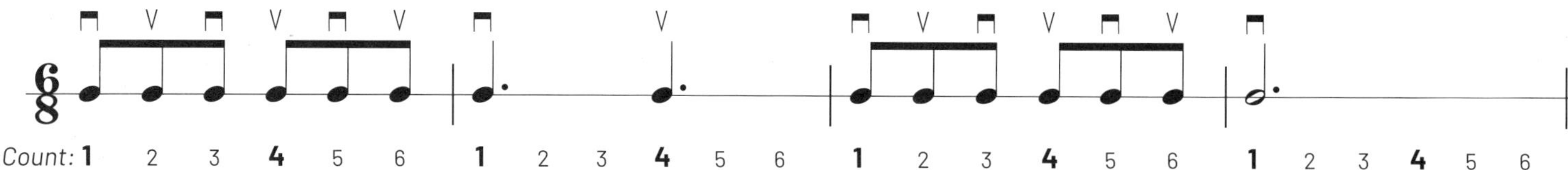

116. LAZY DAY

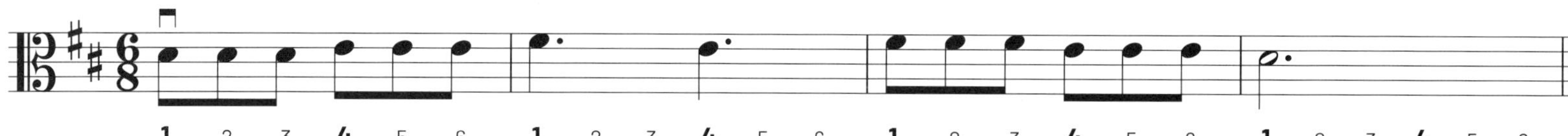

117. HOOKED ON 6/8

THEORY

Musical Form

A round is a **musical form** where performers play or sing the same melody, entering at different times. This is called counterpoint, a type of harmony. Try memorizing this round and performing it with a friend.

118. ROW, ROW, ROW YOUR BOAT – Round

American Folk Round

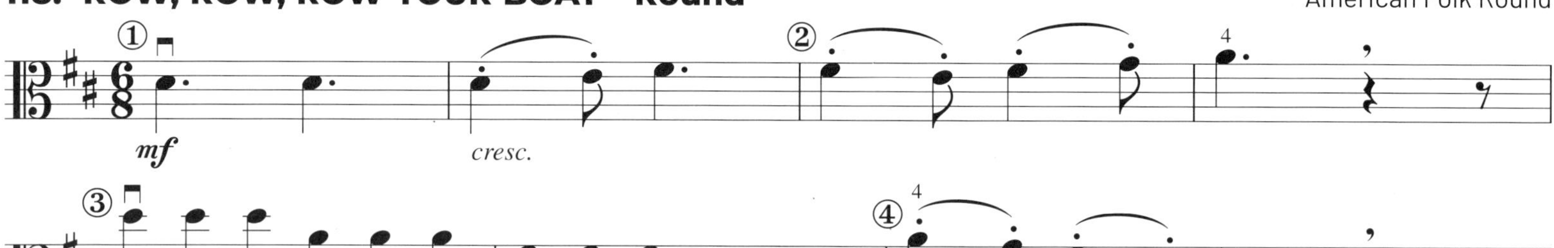

119. SLURRING IN 6/8 TIME

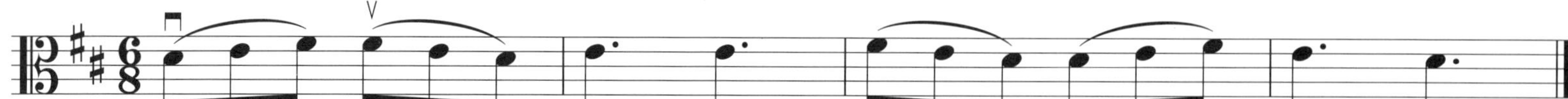

120. JOLLY GOOD FELLOW

THEORY

6/8 Time Signature

When music in 6/8 is played fast, it is easier to stress beats one and four, and "feel" the pulse in two large beats.

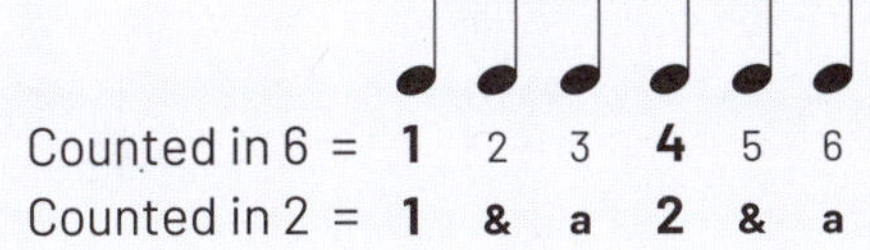
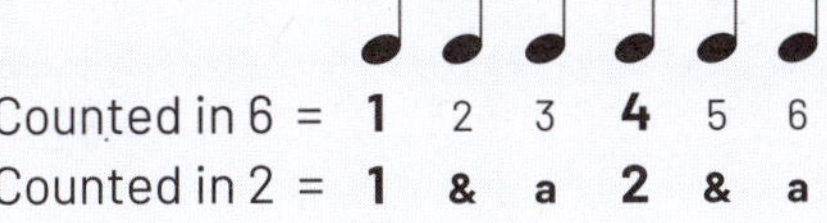

6/8 RHYTHMS

121. RHYTHM RAP

Shadow bow and count before playing.

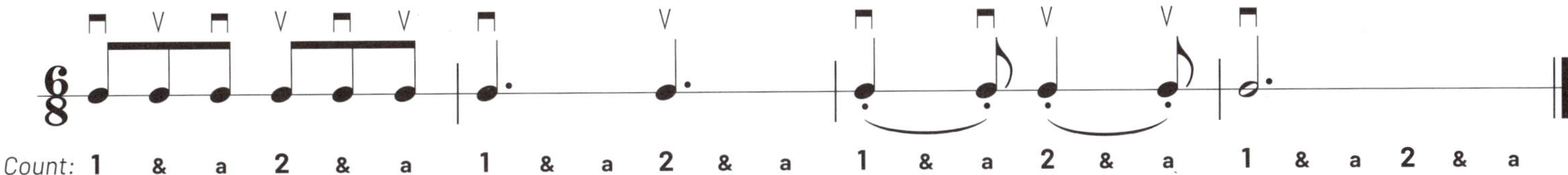

122. RISE AND FALL

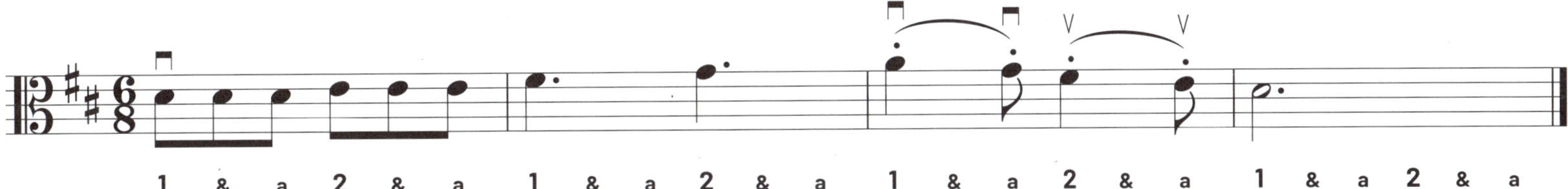

123. BEACH WALK

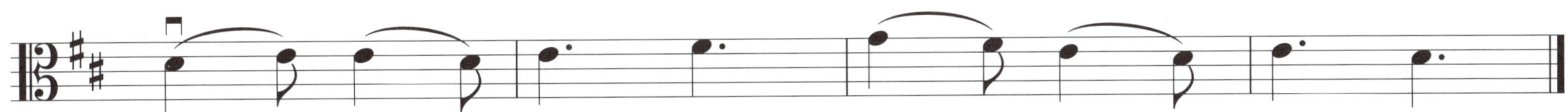

Write in the correct time signature before you begin.

HISTORY

Austrian composer **Wolfgang Amadeus Mozart** was a child prodigy who lived during the American Revolution. At five, he was composing music, and by his early teens he had mastered the violin. Mozart wrote more than 600 compositions during his short life, including oratorios, symphonies, concertos, and operas. Imagine and describe the career of a composer.

124. MAY TIME

W. A. Mozart (1756–1791)

THEORY

Minor Scale

A minor scale is a series of eight notes which follow a definite pattern of whole steps and half steps. There are three forms of the minor scale; natural minor, harmonic minor, and melodic minor. The D minor (natural) scale uses the same pitches as the F major scale.

125. D MINOR (Natural) SCALE

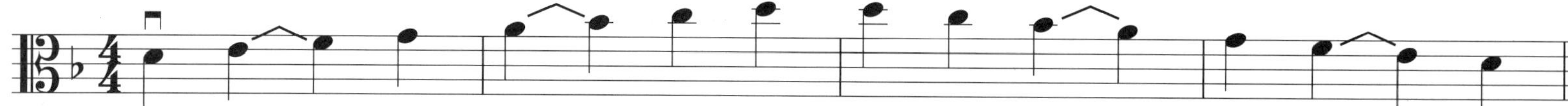

HISTORY

Austrian composer **Gustav Mahler** was also a successful conductor. He believed in unifying the arts and often combined music, poetry, and philosophy in his compositions. Exercise 126 *Mahler's Theme* first appears in his *Symphony No. 1*, played as a solo by the double bass. During Mahler's lifetime Vincent van Gogh created his most famous paintings, and Mark Twain wrote *Tom Sawyer*.

126. MAHLER'S THEME – Round

Gustav Mahler (1860–1911)

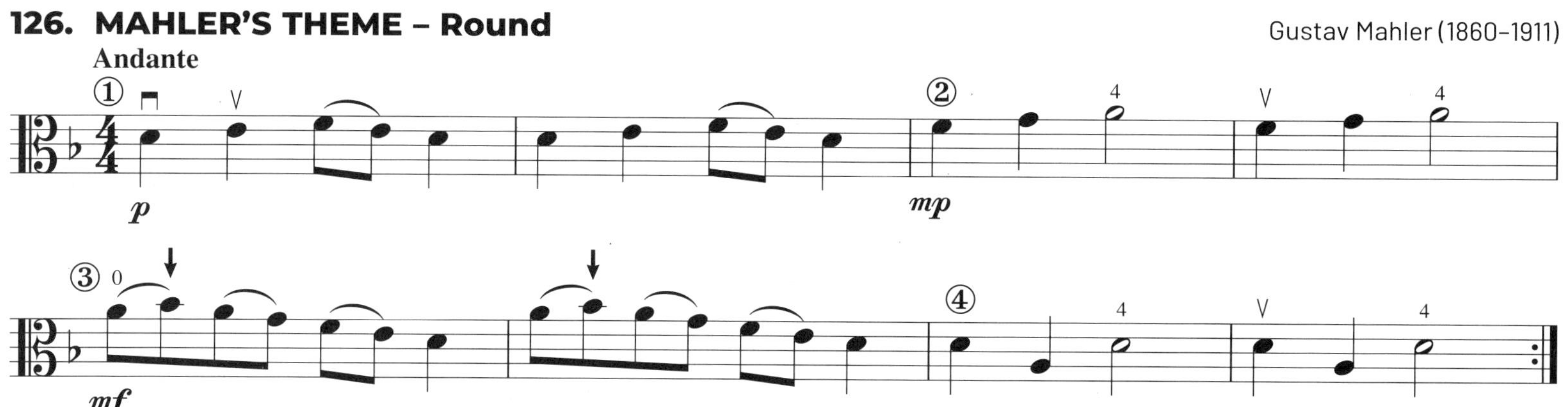

127. SHALOM CHAVERIM – Round

Hebrew Folk Song

128. THE SNAKE CHARMER

Key Signature G MINOR

The G minor (natural) scale uses the same pitches as the B♭ major scale.

129. G MINOR (Natural) SCALE

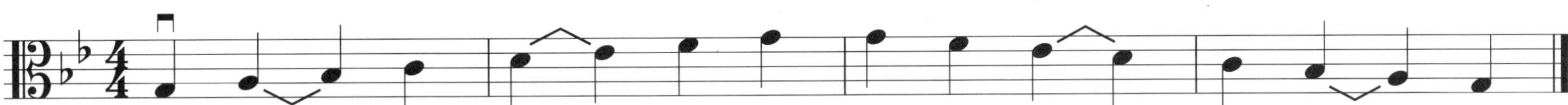

With the establishment of Israel as an independent political state in 1948, *Hatikvah* became the Israeli National Anthem. This was the same year Mohandas Gandhi was assassinated in India. Israeli violinists Itzhak Perlman and Pinchas Zukerman are concert artists known throughout the world.

130. HATIKVAH

Israeli National Anthem

131. G MINOR (Natural) SCALE *(Upper Octave – violin)*

132. ESSENTIAL ELEMENTS QUIZ – THE HANUKKAH SONG

Israeli Folk Song

THEORY

Mixed Meter

Occasionally the meter (time signature) changes in music. Watch for meter changes and count carefully.

MIXED METER

133. RHYTHM RAP

Shadow bow and count before playing.

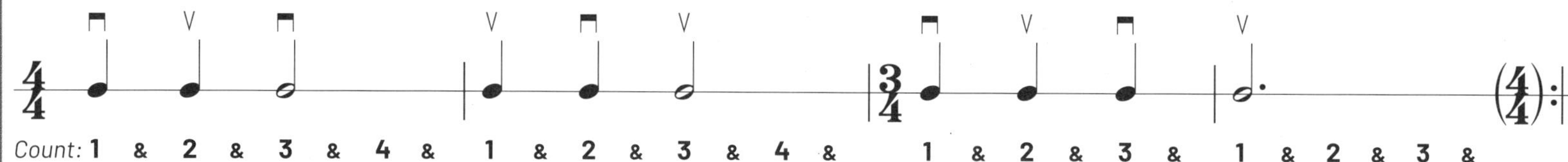

134. FRENCH FOLK SONG

Moderato

THEORY

Cantabile

In a singing style.

e The Italian word for "and."

135. KUM BA YAH

African Spiritual

Andante e cantabile

Triplets

THEORY

A **triplet** is a group of **3** notes. In $\frac{2}{4}$, $\frac{3}{4}$, or $\frac{4}{4}$ time, an eighth note triplet is spread evenly across one beat.

3 = 1 beat

1 trip-let 2 trip-let

RHYTHMS

136. RHYTHM RAP

Shadow bow and count before playing.

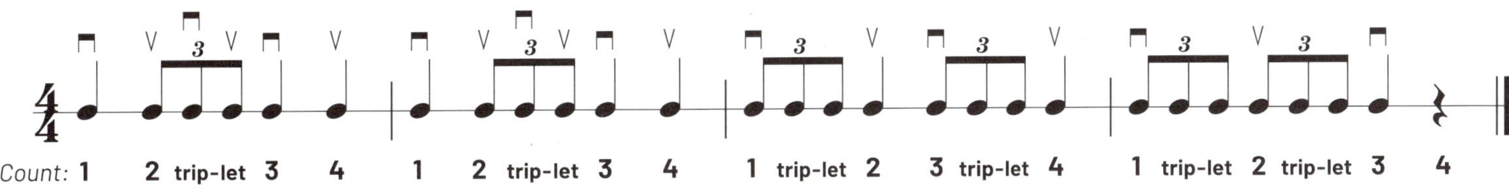

137. D MAJOR SCALE WITH TRIPLETS

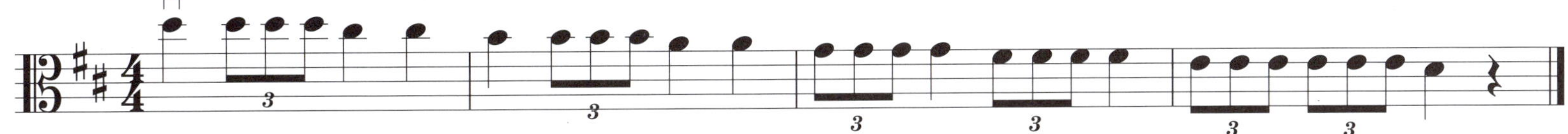

138. ON THE MOVE

139. SLURRING TRIPLETS

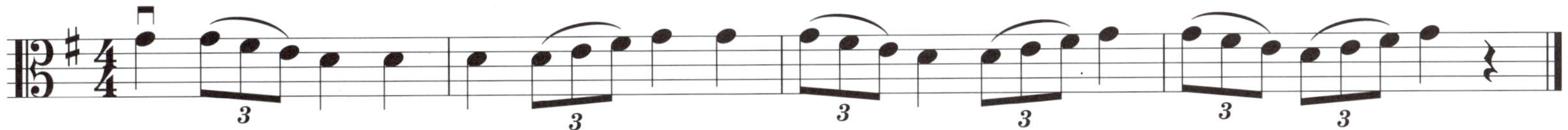

140. TRIPLET ETUDE

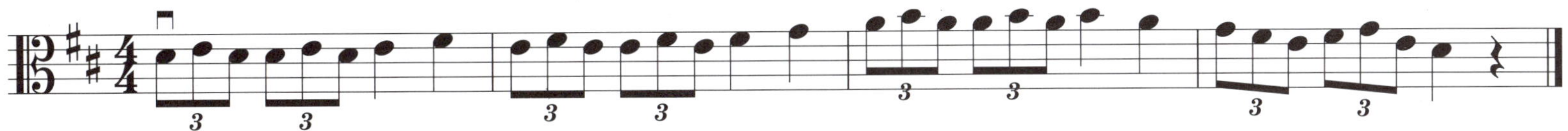

141. LITTLE RIVER

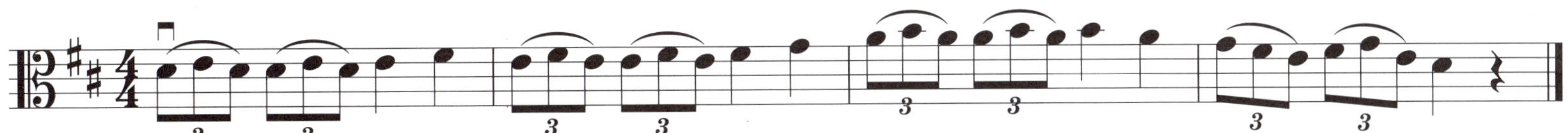

142. FIELD SONG

Southern American Folk Song

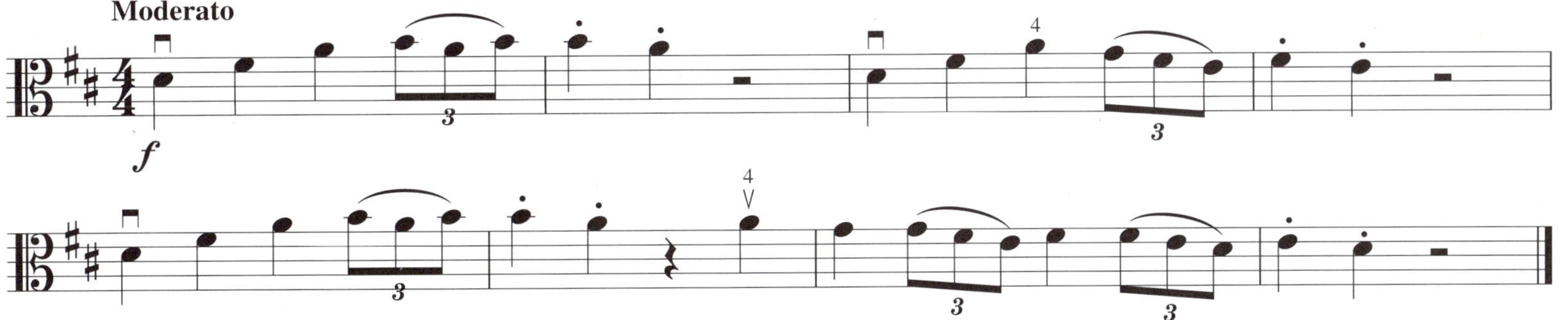

Looking for some more fun music to play?
See the inside front cover for instructions on accessing recent popular Bonus Songs.

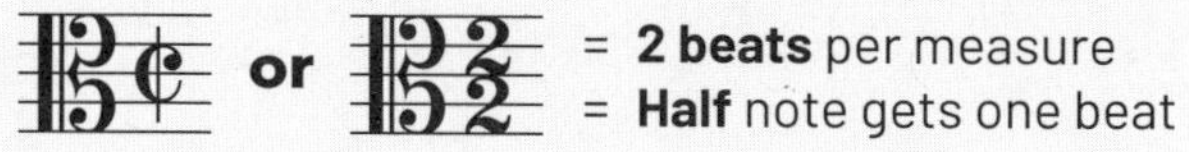

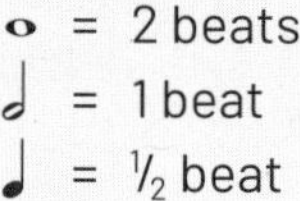

143. RHYTHM RAP

Shadow bow and count before playing.

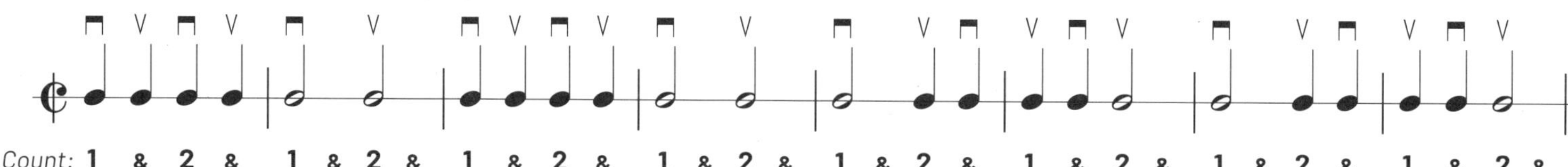

144. A CUT ABOVE

145. CUT TIME MARCH

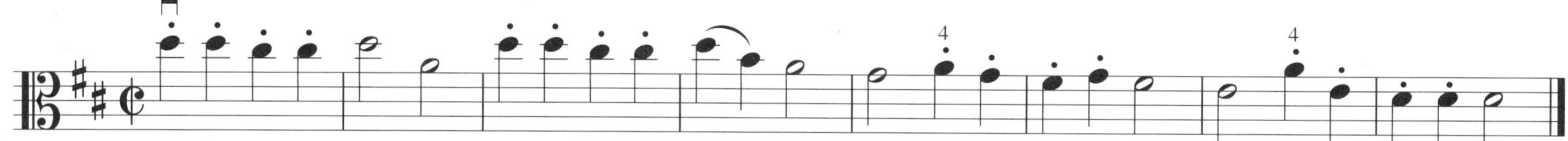

146. RHYTHM RAP

Shadow bow and count before playing.

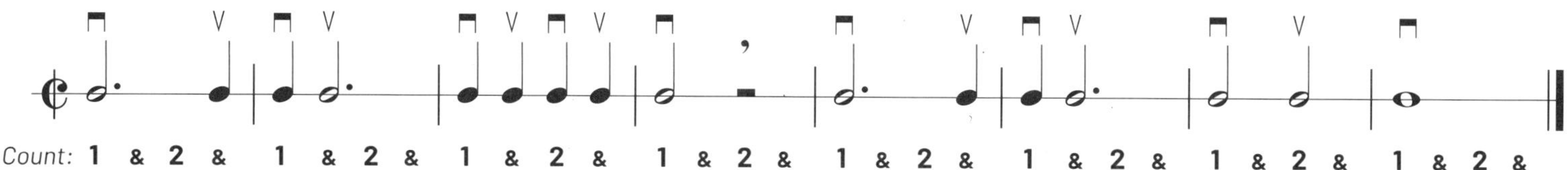

147. SYNCOPATION MARCH

148. WHEN THE SAINTS GO MARCHIN' IN

James M. Black

✔ Are you counting in cut time?

149. RHYTHM RAP

Shadow bow and count before playing.

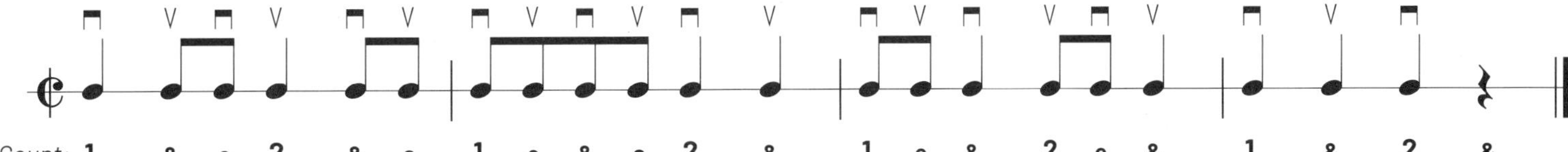

150. DOWN HOME

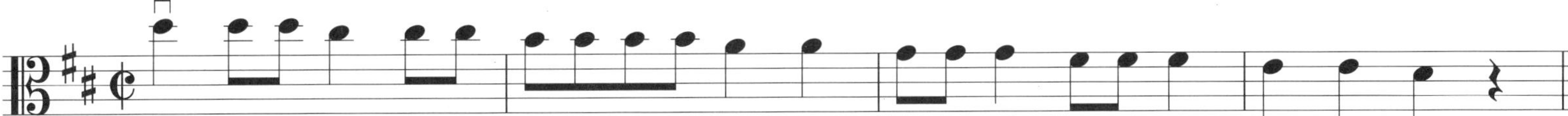

¢ RHYTHMS

151. MOVING ALONG

152. RHYTHM RAP

Shadow bow and count before playing.

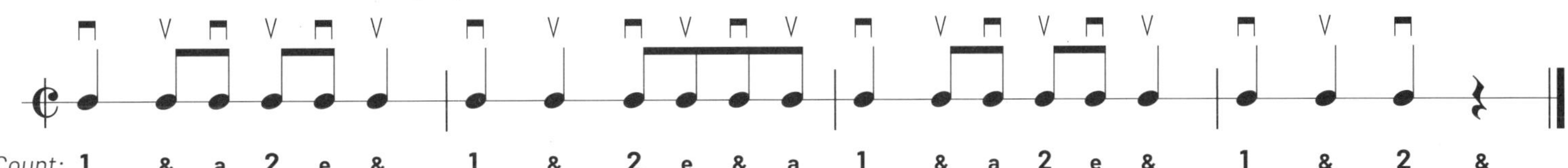

153. UP TOWN

154. FLYING BOWS

HISTORY

Cantatas are pieces much like short operas that were written during the **Baroque Period** (1600–1750). They involve vocal soloists and choirs that are accompanied by small orchestras. **Johann Sebastian Bach** wrote nearly 300 of them between 1704 and 1745. While Bach was composing his cantatas, the famous philosopher Voltaire was writing his books and Thomas Jefferson, the great United States president, was born.

155. MARCH FROM PEASANT'S CANTATA

J. S. Bach (1685–1750)

PERFORMANCE SPOTLIGHT

Performing music for others is fun and rewarding. Either small or large ensembles can perform the following arrangements. Always observe proper concert etiquette by being well prepared, dressing appropriately, being on time, and remembering all equipment. Show respect when others are playing by listening attentively and applauding at the appropriate time.

156. SAGEBRUSH OVERTURE – Orchestra Arrangement A = Melody part. B = Orchestra part.

Arr. John Higgins

Andantino

3 "Streets of Laredo"

A

B

p

mf

11

p

mf

rit. e dim.

Allegretto

mp

23 "Yellow Rose of Texas"

f

✔ What were the strong points of your performance?

157. POMP AND CIRCUMSTANCE – Orchestra Arrangement

Edward Elgar (1857–1933)
Arr. John Higgins

A = Melody part. **B** = Orchestra part.

Moderato

A
B
mp - f
mp - f
1.
2.
11
rit.
rit.

158. AMERICA THE BEAUTIFUL – Orchestra Arrangement

Samuel Augustus Ward (1847–1903)
Arr. John Higgins

A = Melody part. **B** = Orchestra part.

Andante e legato

A
B
mp
mf
9
rit.
f

PERFORMANCE SPOTLIGHT

159. LA BAMBA – Duet

Mexican Folk Song
Arr. Michael Allen

Allegro

A
B

Fine

D.C. al Fine

PERFORMANCE SPOTLIGHT

HISTORY

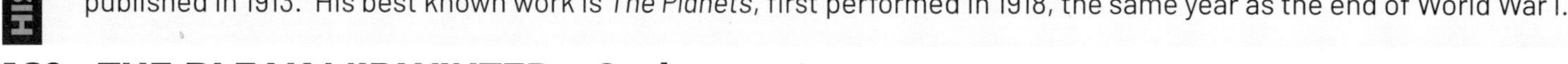

Gustav Holst was a famous British orchestra composer who frequently set words to music, including poems by the American poet, Walt Whitman. Holst's *St. Paul's Suite* for string orchestra was written for the St. Paul's Girls School Orchestra and published in 1913. His best known work is *The Planets*, first performed in 1918, the same year as the end of World War I.

160. THE BLEAK MIDWINTER – Orchestra Arrangement

A = Melody part. **B** = Orchestra part.

Gustav Holst (1874–1934)
Arr. John Higgins

Andante

A
B

rit.

161. SWALLOWTAIL JIG – Orchestra Arrangement

A = Melody part. **B** = Orchestra part.

Irish Jig
Arr. John Higgins

Sight-reading

Sight-reading means playing a musical piece for the first time. The key to sight-reading success is to know what to look for *before* you play. Use the word **S-T-A-R-S** to remind yourself what to look for, and eventually your orchestra will become sight-reading STARS!

S – **Sharps or flats** in the key signature
T – **Time signature** and **tempo markings**
A – **Accidentals** not found in the key signature
R – **Rhythms**, silently counting the more difficult notes and rests
S – **Signs**, including dynamics, articulations, repeats and endings

162. SIGHT-READING CHALLENGE #1

163. SIGHT-READING CHALLENGE #2

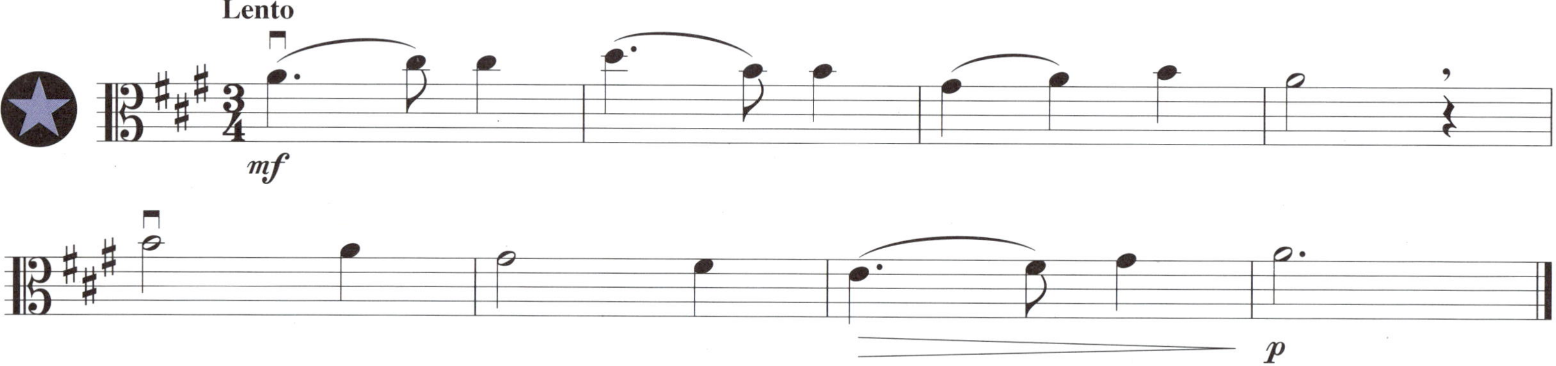

164. SIGHT-READING CHALLENGE #3

165. SIGHT-READING CHALLENGE #4

PREPARING FOR HIGHER POSITIONS

Natural Harmonic

Natural harmonics are tones created by a vibrating string divided into equal sections. To play an octave higher than an open string, lightly touch the string exactly half way between the bridge and the nut. In the following examples, harmonics are indicated by a "o" above a note, plus a fingering number. $\overset{4}{\circ}$ indicates a harmonic played with the fourth finger.

THEORY

Shifting

Sliding your left hand smoothly and lightly to a new location on the fingerboard, indicated by a dash (–). Be sure your thumb moves with your hand.

THEORY

HARMONICS/SHIFTING

FINGER PATTERNS

There are four basic finger patterns, which are combinations of whole and half steps. In the "open" hand pattern, a half step occurs between the open string and first finger. The other patterns have half steps between 1-2, 2-3, or 3-4. Notice that some finger patterns include new notes.

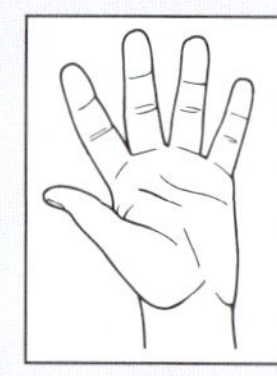

open hand

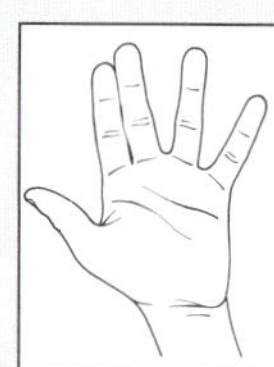

1-2

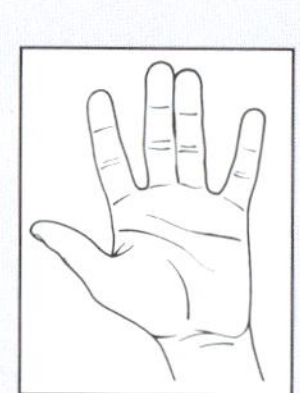

2-3

3-4

FINGER PATTERNS (By Pattern)

174. 3–4 PATTERN

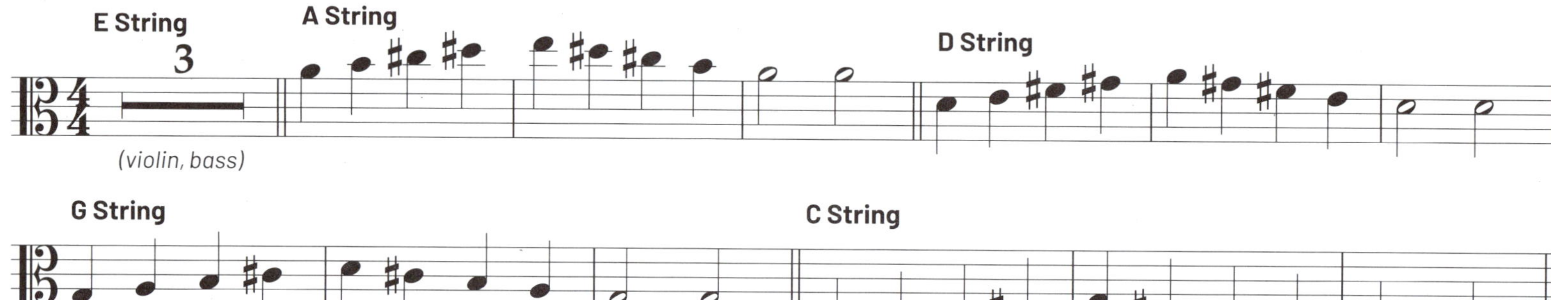

175. 2–3 PATTERN

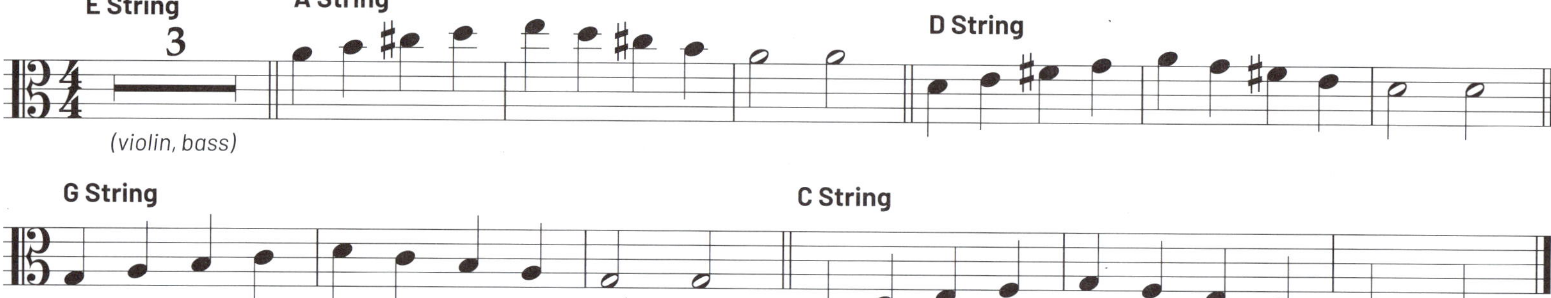

176. 1–2 PATTERN

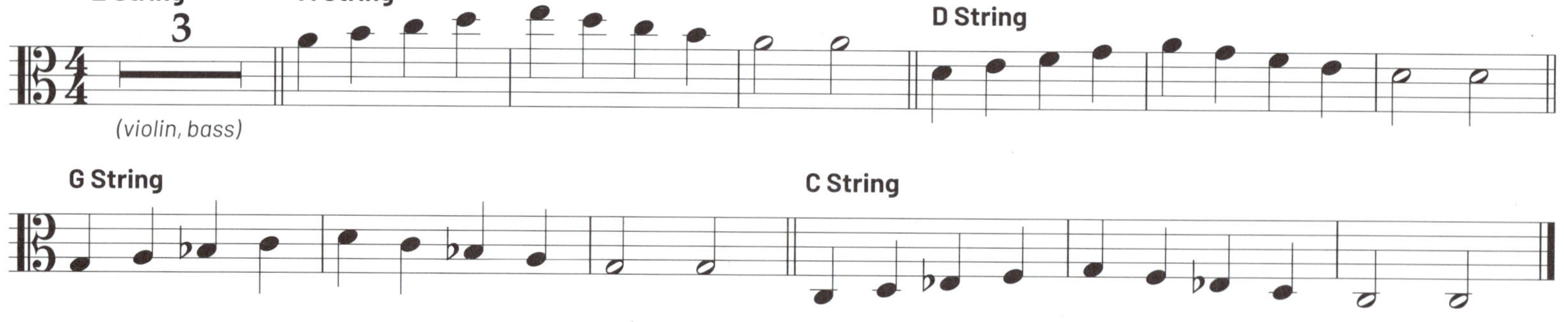

177. OPEN PATTERN

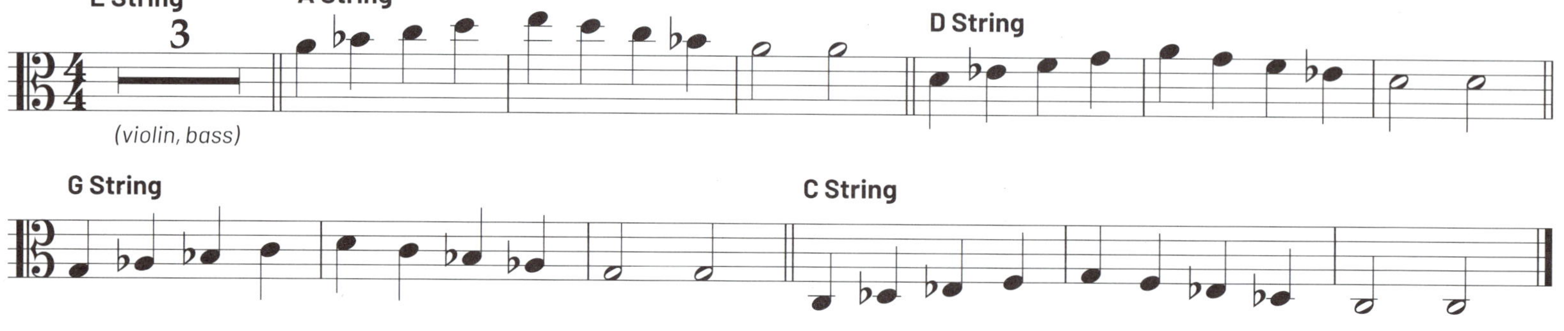

FINGER PATTERNS (By String)

FINGER PATTERNS (By Key)

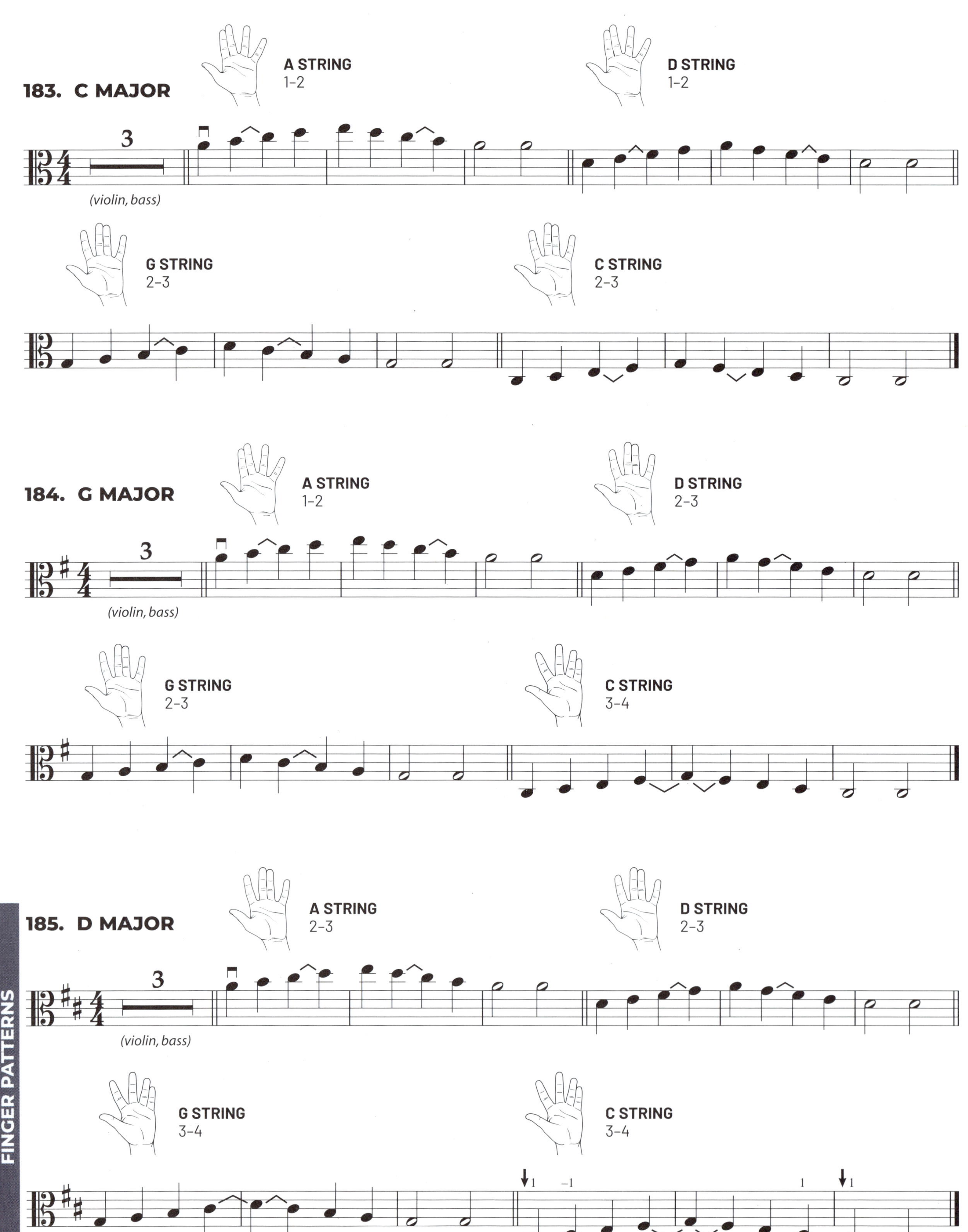

186. A MAJOR

A STRING
2–3

D STRING
3–4

(violin, bass)

G STRING
3–4

C STRING
open hand

187. F MAJOR

A STRING
open hand

D STRING
1–2

(violin, bass)

G STRING
1–2

C STRING
2–3

188. B♭ MAJOR

A STRING
3–4

D STRING
open hand

(violin, bass)

G STRING
1–2

C STRING
1–2

SCALES AND ARPEGGIOS

Identify two important elements of performing scales and arpeggios accurately. As you play each line, check to make sure you are able to do these things.

189. C MAJOR

190. C MAJOR

191. G MAJOR

192. G MAJOR *(Upper Octave – violin)*

193. D MAJOR

194. D MAJOR

195. A MAJOR

196. A MAJOR *(Upper Octave – violin)*

197. F MAJOR

198. B♭ MAJOR

199. B♭ MAJOR *(Upper Octave – violin)*

200. D MINOR (Natural)

201. D MINOR (Natural)

202. G MINOR (Natural)

203. G MINOR (Natural) *(Upper Octave – violin)*

CREATING MUSIC

THEORY

Improvisation

Improvisation is the art of freely creating your own music as you play.

204. *Using the following notes, improvise your own melody (Line A) to go with the accompaniment (Line B).*

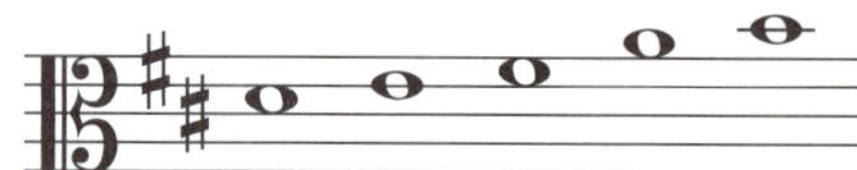

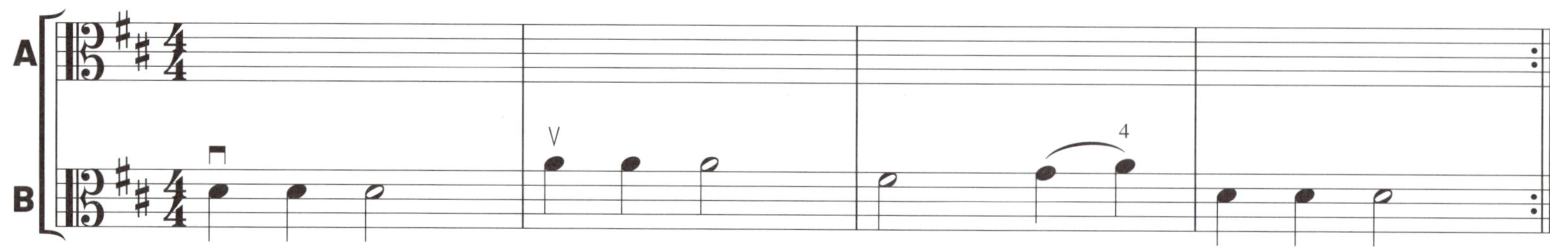

THEORY

Composition

Composition is the art of writing original music. A composer often begins by creating a melody made up of individual **phrases**, like short musical "sentences." Some melodies have phrases that seem to answer or respond to "question" phrases, as in Beethoven's *Ode To Joy*. Play this melody and listen to how phrase 2 answers phrase 1.

205. ODE TO JOY

Ludwig van Beethoven (1770–1827)

206. PHRASE BUILDERS *Write 2 different phrases using the following rhythms.*

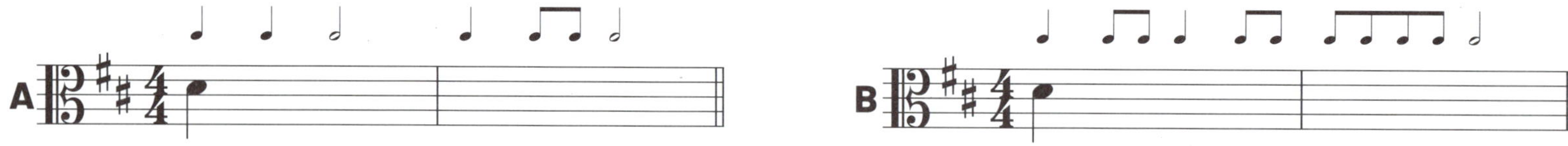

207. Q. AND A. *Write your own "answer" to the following melodies.*

208. YOU NAME IT: ______________________________

Now write your own music.

IMPROVISATION/COMPOSITION

Double Stops

A **double stop** is playing two strings at once.

209. TWO AT A TIME

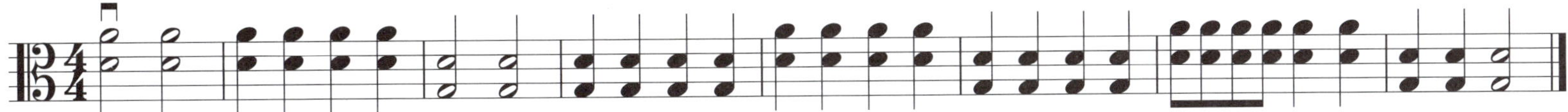

210. ADDING FINGERS

VIOLA FINGERING CHART

A STRING

0	↓1	1	↓2	↑2	3	↓4	4	4 (Harmonic)
A	B♭	B	C	C♯	D	E♭	E	A

Harmonic

D STRING

0	↓1	1	↓2	↑2	3	↑3	4	4 (Harmonic)
D	E♭	E	F	F♯	G	G♯	A	D

Harmonic

G STRING

0	1	↓2	↑2	3	↑3	4
G	A	B♭	B	C	C♯	D

C STRING

0	1	↑2	3	↑3	4
C	D	E	F	F♯	G

Reference Index

Definitions (pg.)

A Tempo 23
Accent 15
Alle Breve 32
Allegretto 6
Andantino 11
Cantabile 30
Cantata 33
Composition 46
Concerto 21
Crescendo *(cresc.)* 3
Cut Time 32
Decrescendo *(decresc.)* 3
Dotted Quarter Note 10
Double Stop 47
Dynamics 3, 7
e 30
Eighth rest 9
Fermata 10
Finger Patterns 40 *(violin & viola)*
Harmonic 39
Improvisation 46
Interval 4
Intonation 5
Legato 2
Lento 11
Meter Change 30
Mezzo piano (***mp***) 7
Mezzo forte (***mf***) 7
Minor Scale 28
Ritardando *(rit.)* 11
Round 26
Sight-reading 38
6/8 26
Sixteenth Notes 16
Shifting 39
Syncopation 19
Triplet 31

Book I Review

Allegro 5
Andante 4
Bow Lift 3
Common Time 7
Dotted Half Note 3
Eighth Note 3
1st & 2nd Endings 3
Forte (***f***) 3
Half Note 2
Hooked Bowing 4
Major Scale 2
Moderato 3
Piano (***p***) 3
Quarter Note 2
Slur 2
Staccato 6
Tie 3
Tone 7
Whole Note 2

Composers

J.S. BACH
- March from "Peasant's Cantata" 33

LUDWIG VAN BEETHOVEN
- Theme from "Violin Concerto in D" 21
- Ode To Joy 46

WILLIAM BILLINGS
- Chester 4

ANTONIN DVORÁK
- Theme from "New World Symphony" 11

EDWARD ELGAR
- Pomp and Circumstance 35

EDVARD GRIEG
- Morning from "Peer Gynt" 3

ALICE HAWTHORNE (SEPTIMUS WINNER)
- Mockingbird 16

FRANZ JOSEPH HAYDN
- Theme from "London Symphony" 2

GUSTAV HOLST
- In the Bleak Midwinter 36

GUSTAV MAHLER
- Theme from "Symphony No. 1" 28

JEAN-JOSEPH MOURET
- Rondeau 11

WOLFGANG AMADEUS MOZART
- May Time 27

JACQUES OFFENBACH
- Barcarolle 3

HENRY PURCELL
- Rigaudon 8

SAMUEL WARD
- America The Beautiful 35

World Music

AFRICAN
- Kum Bah Yah 30

AMERICAN
- America The Beautiful 35
- A Capital Ship 11
- Children's Shoes 19
- Mountain Deer Chase 25
- Field Song 31
- Jesse James 9
- The Streets of Laredo 34
- Tom Dooley 19
- Row, Row, Row Your Boat 26
- When The Saints Go Marching In 32
- Yellow Rose of Texas 34

ENGLISH
- Jolly Good Fellow 26

FRENCH
- At Pierrot's Door 12
- Alouette 8
- French Folk Song 30

HEBREW/ ISRAELI
- Ayn Kaylokaynu 23
- The Hannukah Song 29
- Hatikvah 29
- Shalom Chaverim 28

IRISH
- Rakes of Mallow 25
- Swallowtail Jig 37

MEXICAN
- La Bamba 36

RUSSIAN
- Russian Folk Tune 14
- Sitka City 15

SLOVAKIA
- Slovakian Folk Song 23